Don't Stop
Believing
Our Journey
with Cancer

KASEY CRAWFORD KELLEM

 Halo ●●●●
Publishing International

ISBN: 978-1-61244-379-9
Library of Congress Control Number: 2015949501

Printed in the United States of America

 Published by Halo Publishing International
1100 NW Loop 410
Suite 700 - 176
San Antonio, Texas 78213
Toll Free 1-877-705-9647
Website: www.halopublishing.com
E-mail: contact@halopublishing.com

Dedication

To Craig—Thank you for all of the lessons you taught me on hope, love, perseverance, patience and kindness. Because of you, I have not only changed for good, but I also have changed for the better.

Your faith was perpetual.

Your perseverance was indestructible.

You love was unconditional.

Your trust unalterable.

Your laugh was infectious.

Your patience was unprecedented.

Your courage was dauntless.

Your tenacity was invincible.

Your strength was unbreakable.

Your kindness was contagious.

Your disease was incurable.

Your journey is everlasting.

Index

Chapter One	We Found Love	7
Chapter Two	We Believed	16
Chapter Three	We Lived, Laughed & Loved	21
Chapter Four	We Were Tested	26
Chapter Five	We Were Really Tested	30
Chapter Six	We Were Given Hope	37
Chapter Seven	We Gave Others Hope	44
Chapter Eight	He Took a Risk	50
Chapter Nine	He Didn't Look or Feel Good	57
Chapter Ten	He Was Beat Up, But Not Beat Down	70
Chapter Eleven	We Still Celebrated	75
Chapter Twelve	He Still Believed!	82
Chapter Thirteen	He Threw a Party on His Deathbed	90
Chapter Fourteen	We Celebrated His Life	96
Chapter Fifteen	He Traveled with Me	105
Chapter Sixteen	I Still Believe	113
Chapter Seventeen	I Received	119
	Epilogue	128

Chapter One
We Found Love

Love is the energy of life. ~Robert Browning

Just a small town girl,

Livin' in a lonely world

She took the midnight train

Goin' anywhere

Just a city boy,

Born and raised in South Detroit

He took the midnight train

Goin' anywhere

A singer in a smokey room

The smell of wine and cheap perfume

For a smile they can share the night

It goes on and on and on and on

~Journey

Well, that is somewhat how our love story began, except there wasn't a train, we drove cars. He lived in Cleveland, not Detroit. We did meet in a bar, but only because our mutual friends set us up there. But, the smile we shared that night did go on and on and on and on...even throughout his two, plus year journey with terminal, prostate cancer that metastasized to all of his bones. Our journey is somewhat like other couples experiencing the hardship of disease, but we threw in large doses of optimism, faith and hope, along with A LOT of celebrating. We Believed.

Craig was a broken hearted, divorced, proud father of two tweeners and the co-owner of a large print company, and a few other businesses. At the time, he had reduced his alcohol consumption due to, well, let's just call it an "incident" involving the police and later resulted in him creating a limo company to avoid that situation again. Who does that? This guy!

I was a single, school counselor with ten nieces and nephews, 500 students and zero kids of my own. I was ok with that. After all, I didn't have to give up drinking for ten months to have a kid. Yay, me! I had three wonderful sisters and a father who was forever in love and dedicated to my mother, who passed away a month earlier. They were my inspiration for true love. I yearned, all of my adult life, for what they had for forty-two years and was determined to find it.

I was the Junior Class Advisor, and was having our annual *Prom Show* this particular afternoon that would eventually change my life for good. I had a frantic call from the secretary stating some manager of a limo company wanted to bring his limo to my show that was starting in two hours. I told her to have at it. The more the merrier. At 3:00pm, the manager, Paul, showed up with the limo party bus and we hit it off instantly. We had mutual *smart aleck* personalities, which out-shined one another. Paul was also the father of two of my colleagues/friends at work. Small world!

The story gets a little fuzzy here as neither his daughter, Terri, who was also a part of my elite group of lady friends, "The A-Team" or he would take credit for having the idea to introduce Craig and I. Apparently, later that evening, Paul, as was often the case, was on the phone with Craig. After hanging up, his daughter, who lived at home, and him then had a conversation about fixing us up.

For a month, Terri and my girlfriends from The A-Team attempted to talk me into meeting this man. He was successful, wealthy and really nice. I knew there had to be something wrong with him and I was contently settled into my pathetic single life. I was going to be that crazy aunt who spoiled all the nieces and nephews, and left big red lipstick kiss marks on their cheeks every time I saw them. I didn't wear lipstick, but I was willing to start…at some point. But, I finally caved in and agreed to meet said "successful, wealthy, nice man" at their relative's bar.

Craig was drinking coke, as he did not drink and drive, and since it was a school night, Thursday, I too was not imbibing. We hit it off instantly sharing a common interest in golfing, skiing and socializing. He actually asked me for a kiss and a hug when he walked me to the car and explained he was an affectionate person. I gave in—seriously, I was DYING for affection! He asked me out...on a date…which I had never been on in my thirty-eight years of life. Pathetic. Yes, I had boyfriends; we just never went on romantic dates. WTH?

At the time, I had moved away from my small, suburban community to get away from a few of the men I previously dated. I was living in some country-like community about thirty minutes away from any familiar suburbs. I barely knew any of my neighbors, as I was certain we lacked anything in common. I lived there for one reason, my home backed up to the sixth hole of a golf course. Sold.

Craig picked me up in one of his limos from his Silver Spoon Limo Company. Imagine the looks on the faces of my hillbilly, gun-toting, rig-driving neighbors when they saw this shiny white, long stretch limo picking up the new girl in the hood. As soon as I entered the limo, he announced, "Today is the two year anniversary of my mother's death!" I quickly responded, "Wow! It is the one month anniversary of my mother's death." I then went on to explain to him that I was certain my mother got up to Heaven and asked around to see if anyone had a nice son for her loser daughter to date. TAH-DAH! Thank you Doris and Shorty, you girls did well!

Craig and I went to Johnny's on Fulton, truly one of the finest restaurants in Cleveland and then to a comedy show. I ordered the whole hog dinner, well, my nickname for the "Italian Feast" that looked like something Fred Flintstone would order. *She's a keeper!* I thought as I indulged. We then headed to a comedy show. Our conversation flowed smoothly the entire evening. Craig was very proud of his daughter, Jessica and son, Joe. He bragged about them while I envisioned becoming a stepmother. A perfect night in my books!

At the time, I had three brother-in-laws. Each called the day of the big date and independently told me that I could not have sex with this man on my first date. Since they all knew my *dateless* track record it was imperative this message be relayed to me and that I fully understand any and all ramifications that may occur if I cave in to my libido that evening. Geez, I had cobwebs for crying out loud! UGH!

I listened and although we affectionately kissed in the back of the limo on the way home, I informed him about the advice of my three brother-in-laws. What a buzz and testosterone kill conversation that was. Craig was a clever and creative man, one with great problem-solving skills. Who am I kidding the man was as lonely and sexually deprived as I was. He was back at my door the next morning with flowers and the remainder of our Champaign from the night before. In my defense, I didn't have sex with Craig on our first date. I was in love!

We hit it off from the very beginning enjoying our time golfing, skiing and socializing, though we were the greatest at the latter. He was very protective of his kids and didn't want them to meet me early in the relationship. I completely understood and agreed. In fact, he told me that he could not even consider marrying me until his kids graduated from high school. They were both in the 7th grade. Being a bit of a free spirit, I rather liked this new life style. I saw him Tuesdays, Thursdays and every other weekend, and played with my girl friends on the nights he had his kids. I could easily do this for five more years. Yahooey!

That plan didn't last for long. Two years later, he asked me to marry him. We married six months later, after his kids finished the 9th grade. I was a stepmother. Suddenly, more than ever, my bachelor, master and educational specialist degrees in special education and counseling would come in handy. My stepson had some special needs and I had big plans for how I was going to help him. My stepdaughter was like me without my DNA— good student, good athlete, *familiar* with the judicial system and VERY outgoing. How the heck does this happen? I know exactly how. My mother said for years, "I hope you have a child just like you!" Her damn curse worked. But, I was still feeling very blessed.

So there I was —forty, married and a stepmom living in a beautiful suburban home. This was truly something I dreamt about for years. I couldn't believe my dream actually came true! I couldn't have been any happier or fulfilled. I had a husband who loved me unconditionally, treated me with the utmost respect, was more fun than any person I ever knew and kept up with my drinking. Or was it the other way around? We were so in love and blessed. This man even accepted me despite me being do-mestically inept AND directionally challenged, something that would probably bother any other man.

We laughed. We laughed a lot. We had our inside jokes and did things to each other probably not done under other roofs. My favorite was when Craig would just randomly poke me anywhere anytime, accompanied directly by a long, obnoxious and almost often smelly fart. Where most wives would find this disgusting, I giggled incessantly. He would wake me from a sound sleep in the middle of the night with his poke, let out his explosion and I would giggle myself back to sleep. Now, if you knew my husband who stood 6 feet 1 inch tall, weighing over 200 pounds, often sporting a suit jacket and rather debonair looking (at least in my eyes), this kind of behavior seemed uncanny of him. No matter what the circumstance, he always got a laugh out me when he did that.

I would always say, "I heard that," to him if he burped. No matter how far away I was, I always heard his burping and softly said, "I heard that," which made us giggle because of the root of that saying. When I was a child, I was upset with my older sister and called her an "F---ing bitch!" My mother walked by the steps and very sweetly said, "I heard that." Sometimes my mother just got it. Craig really enjoyed that story and somehow that became our line. Even better, he started beating me to the line. He would burp and say aloud to himself, "I heard that," or "Did you hear that," again putting me in a fit of laughter.

His patience was that of a saint. No matter how socially obnoxious I got, he found amusement in my behavior. I often made-up my own jokes and was solely convinced I was super duper funny. Even though Craig knew the obvious punch line, he gave me the moment to shine and the time to deliver my funny joke. I would often have to remind him how funny I was, to which he would kindly respond, "Yes, dear!" It was endearing. And, I was kinda funny...just saying.

Neither of us thought the other was a good driver. He was slow, inattentive and often merged into the adjacent lane...*way*... too late. I was in a hurry to get nowhere, directionally challenged and ADHD. The continuous six points on my license speaks for itself. Hey, my father is a race car driver. I never learned about speed limits! One of Craig's trademarks was to make left turns RIGHT IN FRONT OF oncoming traffic, often times making me almost soil my pants. Since we didn't fight or yell and often just found humor in one another's idiosyncrasies, I figured I might as well just have fun with this. So, I started plastering my face against my passenger window with looks of horror much like Macaulay Culkin in *Home Alone*! We both found great humor in my dramatic window-smashed face, not to mention the reactions of the oncoming drivers who were screeching to avoid our car. Oh, Craigee!

Craig and I enjoyed *Comedy Central*, especially *South Park*, being the intellects that we were. We later enjoyed other mind riveting shows like *Bob's Burgers* and *Bojack the Horseman*, both Netflix cartoon series that we completed in record time. Until his last year of life when he took a liking to *Ellen* and *American Idol*, we really didn't share any other common interest in television shows. I needed humor and he enjoyed *SyFy*, *The History Channel* and *Fox News*. Thankfully, my ADHD prohibited me from spending too many minutes in one place, so Craig ruled the television. Again, not being a couple who argued, I took the liberty always jokingly to tell him, "You watch awful TV!" Craig took over that line, too and would state, "I watch awful TV," as soon as I would come near the family room. His reverse psychology was killing my comedic game. No matter what we did or where we went, Craig kept me laughing.

Craig was a romantic who claimed himself a "male chauvinist" in the sweetest of ways, insisting on paying for fine dining and excursions, but letting me pay for an occasional lunch at the local saloons. He opened doors, walked me to my car every visit and even throughout our marriage up until he couldn't walk. He bought flowers weekly, placing one rose in our bedroom for me, and a bouquet in our kitchen for all to enjoy. He started this tradition with Jessica and carried it on with me.

He even sang me lullabies at night just as he had his little girl, along with other romantic songs. His phone messages, many of which I saved, were always positive, sweet and funny even at times when I may have inadvertently left for work with his set of car keys...a few times.

We spent the next few years golfing at the country club, skiing at our ski house in New York and traveling often. We entertained and celebrated anything we could find worth celebrating. We went to baseball games in his lodge, basketball games in his suite and football games in his 50-yard line seats that were forty-two steps away from the bar. His children and friends quickly merged with my friends and family, and we were all one big happy bunch of "Classholes" as I affectionately named us. Those were truly the times of our lives! I was bountiful, blessed, grateful, fulfilled and happier than I had ever been in my life.

Chapter Two
We Believed

Believe in fresh starts and new beginnings. ~Unknown

Prior to becoming a school counselor, I had the pleasure of being a special education teacher and worked under a principal who had been my former teacher, and a nun. By pleasure, I mean..."Crap, I shouldn't have been such a jack wagon in high school because this stuff comes back to bite you!" Thankfully, after hiring me to teach Severe Behaviorally Handicapped kids, because I was "SBH" in her eyes, the former Sr. Gretchen came to love me...in my eyes. After eight years of working with Gretchen, she gave me a *Believe* stone upon my departure. That stone went with me to each of my offices thereafter.

I often found myself fumbling with this *Believe* stone in my palm; wondering why she chose to give that rock to ME. Of course, I believed. I was raised by the most optimistic and positive parents there were. My mother's motto: "If this is the worst thing that ever happened to you, aren't you lucky!" I'm not going to lie, there were times I wanted to scream when she said that to me, like when I broke my hand twice during track season (less related to track and more related to alcohol, and yes this was in high school....don't judge). I also remember her saying it to me when I was juggling three jobs and taking twenty-one credit hours in college. Don't have pity on me. That was after a two and half year vacation at Ohio University where I spent more time traveling with the *Grateful Dead* and socializing than I ever did learning and studying. My dear little Italian mother always found a way to "comfort" me with those words. She believed. I believed. I had that stone from Gretchen as a gentle reminder.

Craig was going through a heartbreaking divorce. Heartbreaking to anyone who knows him, since he was such a kind-hearted and loving man. Apparently, one afternoon, he was crying while looking out his kitchen window. He was saying to himself, "Why, God, why me?" His daughter, Jessica, was in the bathroom when she belted out, "Hey Daddy, you know what one of my spelling words is? BELIEVE! Wanna here me spell it? B-E-L-I-E-V-E!" It was at that point, Craig stopped feeling victim and started believing he would get through those circumstances and all other challenges that followed.

When we met, he told me this story and somehow *Believe* just became our mantra from then on. I honestly don't remember if there were any signs, plaques or pictures in his house that said, "Believe." I can assure you *Believe* donned the house once I moved in. Like anyone with slight, self-diagnosed OCD, I maybe overdid it with the *Believe* trinkets, but people certainly got the message very quickly when they walked into any room of our home.

The first person really to be affected by this mantra was our friend and cleaning lady, Lidia. She came into our home after Craig and I married, so she didn't know either of our history. We looked like the perfect family—two parents, two kids, big house and even the white picket fence in the front. For real. The only thing missing was a cute little puppy, like a pit bull, which came later in our love story.

Poor Lidia dusted around every darn *Believe* decoration in our home. It was on our mantle, our bookshelves, the coffee table, in our bedroom, our offices—everywhere. You really couldn't go anywhere in our home and not see the word, "Believe." She didn't understand what we had to *believe* in as we seemingly had a perfect life.

One day Lidia informed me she was getting a divorce and wouldn't be able to clean our house the following week. I sat down with her and told her Craig and my story. She had no idea. I told her, "If I can get a Craigee, anyone can! You just have to *believe*." From that day on, Fridays became HER day. She looked forward to cleaning our home while delicately cleaning each and every *Believe* trinket in our home. Soon we became friends and she often stayed and swam with us afterwards.

She also started going out on Fridays and it didn't take long for her to meet her "Craigee." Pat was a perfect gentleman and was quickly welcomed into our family and group of friends. He opened the door for her, bought her flowers and adorned her with affection—a true Craigee! They married and continued to live a happy life together.

My dear friend and colleague, Bick also faced some heartbreak and challenges. We often met in my office and talked about her getting back on her feet with three children, including a newborn. Despite the pain of her divorce, I kept encouraging her to believe. She did. And guess what? She found herself a "Craigee," too!

It was an interesting twist of fate that when I met Craig I was helping Shelley, a Senior Cosmetology student in high school diagnosed with sarcoma cancer. It was incurable and her life changed forever after losing her right arm to the disease. One Friday, her mother called to tell me about the upcoming amputation. I tried counseling her best I could. "Believe you will get through this," was part of the discussion, but more importantly, I told this "elderly" sounding woman who I had never met before (turned out to be a hot, young, Barbie-looking mom) that she needed to imbibe that weekend. She assured me she would and I agreed to do the same. I returned to work on Monday to my dear Shelley greeting me with a bottle of Two Buck Chuck, A Trader Joe's classic wine, from her mother. I just knew I was going to love this family and we would be life-long friends.

We gathered every Friday together while Shelley was being tutored, every time she was in the hospital and throughout her times recovering from surgeries and treatments. I continued to encourage them to believe they would all get through this. Their mantra was "Stay Strong!" We sold thousands of bracelets with this mantra, had haircut-a-thons, and the biggest fundraiser I have ever attended, all to buy her some new arms. Arms are cosmetic, you know, says the insurance companies who had an arm to write that clause. Insert frown face.

This family became one of Craig and my closest friends. We cheered Shelley on and continued to believe she would get through it all. And, she did, even with an additional set back a few years later with more cancer in her shoulder and lungs. She still stayed strong, believed and persevered. She married at what was the most emotional wedding my family and friends ever attended. We all believed in Shelley. Little did I know that Shelley would end up being one of Craig's biggest cheerleaders during his bout with cancer. My how life can change in the blink of an eye!

And, the stories go. One by one, friends were going through difficult times, life-changing challenges, life-threatening diseases, adversities, and one worse than the next. Friends divorcing, friends having their children or parents pass away, friends losing their jobs, oh, the list goes on and on and on. But, we continued to encourage them to believe. They continued to persevere. They all turned the beat around and became our biggest cheerleaders during Craig's most challenging time.

Chapter Three
We Lived, Laughed & Loved

The more you praise and celebrate your life,
the more there is in life to celebrate ~Oprah Winfrey

Oh man, did we ever live our lives to the fullest. We may have only had nearly eleven years together, but we packed it full like that of a sixty-year-long couple. We put the "up" in Couple. We were very upbeat and up on each other. Neither of us would ever get upset with the other. My husband and I were amongst the few who found each other amusing and entertaining while others may have found us outright obnoxious. We went to really nice places and were sometimes slightly cut off, given the bill before asking and/or quietly escorted to our limo.

My favorite day of the week was Saturday, not because I got to sleep in, but because I was able to play with Craig all day long. Only Craig could make grocery shopping and errand running the highlight of my week. He would run away with the cart and hide from me at the grocery store. Knowing I was always cold in the store, he took great pride in pushing me into the walk-in cooler each time we passed it. We may have been the only people who found humor in shopping.

I spent a few years making excuses for why we needed to head into the neighboring suburb, which was the home of my favorite little saloon. I pretended to need building supplies from Home Depot, fresher produce from the other grocery store, pool toys in January, garden supplies in February in Cleveland, you name it, all for the sake of getting to ZZ's Saloon. Oh ZZ's, we loved the ZZ's! It was a shot and a beer kind of neighborhood bar that we didn't have in our uppity neighborhood. We got to know the bartenders well, and of course, Craig already knew the owner from years before. We were weekend regulars where, like in *Cheers*, they had our drinks ready for us as soon as we entered. Craig was very particular about his drinks, insisting the cranberry in his vodka and cranberry, and the coke in his rum and coke were only for color. It was almost comical how he was insistent about this wherever we went. One time our regular bartender barked back at him, "Hey, you've never left here not feeling any pain...come to think of it, I don't think you've ever walked in here not feeling any pain!" Damn the gig was up. She had our number. We loved her.

I also loved Thursdays in the summer, as those were Craig's golf daze...um...I mean days. Craig often entertained his employees or other businessmen at the country club or other local golf courses. I had the pleasure of being their "Designated Driver." Where other wives may have been annoyed by the drunken nonsense, I was highly entertained and the next morning I would recap with *great detail* the antics from the previous afternoon, as I was the only sober one there. Watching very successful and wealthy men get hammered and stumble out of the golf course was highly entertaining. Having servers strategically seat us away from anyone else at the restaurants was almost gratifying. Being asked to leave without paying the bill was somewhat insulting as they had money, but sometimes the servers were willing to pay the price just to get us out of their establishment. Those were good times, indeed.

Craig and I were very cultured, well, as cultured as a Westside Clevelander could be. We not only attended all of the professional sporting events, but we actually went to musicals and plays downtown. We laughed and had a great time at each and every one of them, often inviting a crew of friends to join us. Before one particular show, we ran into a young man we had many drinks with over the previous five years. He was a wealthy lawyer and businessman who did business with Craig and knew him from the country club. He introduced us to his friends as, "Two of my oldest friends." It didn't take much time for us to both realized that as he only knew us for a few years, his term "oldest" was directly related to our age. Sigh. We were hanging out with many people twenty-plus Craig's junior, but hey, we were having fun!

We were ten to twenty years older than MANY of the people with whom we entertained. Several of these young men referred to Craig as their "Coach!" He was their drinking coach, rarely sitting on the sidelines, often a hands-on teacher. These men loved, admired and looked up to Craig even though some of them were born with silver spoons in their mouths. Michael, the man who coined the term, "Coach," became another son to Craig and me. He often visited while seeking personal and professional advice from his confidante. He was like a brother to the kids, as well. Coach was the mentor to many and took good care of these boys often taking them golfing, drinking, dining, drinking, skiing, drinking, swimming, and did I mention, drinking. After one night of shots, tequila to be specific, Coach told the boys he was hanging up his cleats and coaching from the sidelines. That lasted until he had the best hangover game of golf the next day. He decided then maybe he just needed never to do tequila again. Good choice, Coach!

Then came the "Sisters," Dean and Dylan, who were really twin brothers nicknamed that back in middle school. They, along with their partner in crime, Forrest, all former students of mine, became the younger cadets of Coach's team. It began with these young track stars coming to our home to do their annual mulch laying fundraiser. Their parents drove them as we lived pretty far from their designated mulching areas. They made an exception for us. Craig paid well. They met Coach and loved him. We socialized with their parents while they prepared our flowerbeds. I knew we had more lifelong friends with their families, too.

Forrest was rather obnoxious (pot calling kettle black) and made certain to torment me daily at school. One day in January of his senior year, he was annoyed I was once again attending a major sporting event not knowing anything about the sport or the famous players. He gave me a proposition, one that would change our lives and relationships forever. He asked if I would take the twins and him to a Cleveland Indians Game in the summer if he acted "normal," good and well behaved the rest of the year. Ha! I scoffed and told him not only would I take them to the game, but I'd also take them in a limo…because it ain't happening. Did I mention it was January and we had FIVE more months of school? There was no way he could make it a week, let alone five months. The next day Forrest showed up with a three-page contract attached to a manila folder and a box of donuts to seal the deal. A daily behavior chart was immediately posted in my office. Alerted, Craig prepared the suite and limo for the unlikeliness of this summer event to occur.

So, there we were, in a limo with these boys and their parents going to an Indians game that June. An added bonus to the excursion was Jessica and her cute, fun girl friends. The bond had grown. Forrest ended up doing an internship with Craig and often times the boys came in town from college just to have lunch with Craig at the local saloon. Coach was a true inspiration to them, not just because of his business success, but also his drinking ability. He was quite the role model. These boys wanted someday to take over Craig's business when he retired and even took a few pictures of themselves in front of his business sign, altering it to say, "Watt (and Sons)." Craig had that effect on the young and the old.

Chapter Four
We Were Tested

*If you want to feel rich just count all the things you have
that money cannot buy.* ~Unknown

Let the good times roll. And we did! We WERE the party! We brought everyone together. We had a blast! We were Livin' La Vida Loca! Oh, the places we went…the people we saw! Oh, S#!^ WE ARE IN A RECESSION!

My husband, with his 180 electoral hours from OSU, co-owned three small, but successful businesses. Apparently, that president, "He who shall not be mentioned by name" in fear my husband will rain on me, didn't hold loving feelings for the small business owners and boy did my husband feel the disdain. For the first time ever, I heard my husband yell. And by "yell," I mean scream bloody murder! One afternoon I found myself double stepping downstairs to the family room to fight off the intruder attacking my husband, only to find him screaming at the television where "He who shall not be mentioned by name" was speaking. In retrospect, I should have jumped out the window, as I could offer no help whatsoever. I couldn't believe my eyes OR my ears. My dear, patient, loving, kind-souled husband, who never raised his voice to his children or me, was screaming out of breath to the TELEVISION! My poor neighbors probably think this sweet man was verbally abusive to all of us.

For the first time, I saw a different side of Craig. He was mad. He was hurt. He was scared. He was screwed! Competitors near and far were closing their print shops. His twenty-five year print company had to make employee cuts, which broke his heart. They were a family of 100 that slowly dwindled to about 60. That is a lot of family to lose in a few short years. His partners and he took major pay cuts. Times were tough and we were feeling it.

Despite Craig choosing to watch *Fox News* each afternoon to "unwind" from his day and scream at "you know who," he still maintained his, "This too shall pass," attitude. We still partied, entertained, attended sports' events and traveled, though now using our millions of accumulated Marriott and Continental points. We somehow still maintained our lifestyle, though with some tweaking. The only thing he would not do was take me to Italy—my "Bucket List" dream trip. He insisted, understandably so, that going to Europe after letting go of forty percent of his employees would be a real slap in the face to his employees, even if I paid for the entire trip. That is what a humble, caring and compassionate business owner he was. We continued to live a very blessed life. In fact, he kept me in the dark enough that while he was downstairs yelling at "you know who," I was upstairs investing my savings into a few ideas, inventions and children's books.

It began with GOLFO, the Bingo golf game the whole family could play—or just your drunk golf buddies. I'm sure you have heard of it. No, oh, that's because it never really took off. Oops, there went a few thousand dollars. How about the "Speak and Post" invention that was going to make us billionaires? Don't have one of those either? Yah that invention company took my money and left me hanging. Where was *Shark Tank* when I needed them? Now, you must have heard about the beloved *Mind Over Matter* children's books that I wrote? Guess the title of the first book...go ahead...you got it...*Believe*! There are five M.O.M. books: *Believe; Love; Relax; Laugh;* and *Dream* only the first three are in print, um, because apparently IT COSTS MONEY TO GO TO PRINT! Who knew? Not this wife of a printer. Yep, I was upstairs investing my savings into all sorts of fun stuff while listening to the now-oh-so-familiar buzzing from my husband downstairs. I was rather clueless of the effect this recession was having on my husband's well-being.

He seemed to spend a lot of time in what we later called, "His depression chair," a worn out recliner. His buddies and he burned, shot and exploded (that's legal, right) the chair one afternoon after Craig finally succumbed to the circumstances. He later realized the stress he induced on himself during this great recession just might have been in part the cause of his cancer. Damn it to hell "He who shall not be mentioned by name!"

To add insult to injury...a few injuries...I learned my falling down sober was not the residual effect of my drinking, but instead from MS. And contrary to my initial years with this diagnosis, MS did NOT stand for "More Shots," but instead stood for Multiple Sclerosis which for me caused bladder issues, inflammation, memory issues (what?) and a major imbalance on my left leg, which I affectionately named, "Nelly." Nelly was a bitch. If I went one way, she went the other or just didn't go at all. She especially didn't take too kindly to the shots of Crown I did on the weekends, but it would take me a few years to figure that one out. Craig often thought that the day would soon come when he would be pushing me in a wheel chair, we would need the stair lift to get me upstairs and he would be caring for my bed-wetting, memory-losing, highly medicated self. Boy, did the tables quickly turn on that one.

In June of 2011, Craig came home from his routine doctor appointment and stated something about his PSA being slightly elevated, but it was nothing to worry about—just a false positive. Not knowing what a PSA was or quite honestly, what purpose the prostate even served, I dismissed the discussion as quickly as Craig did. That summer seemed to be rather normal with the usual parties, golfing and traveling, however that summer, in hindsight, was the beginning of the end.

Chapter Five

We Were Really Tested

*I have never had to face anything that could
overwhelm the native optimism and stubborn
perseverence I was blessed with.* ~Sonia Sotomayor

We were enjoying a great season of skiing by heading to our place in Ellicottville, New York, nearly every weekend that winter. Craig had the trips down to every detail: leave at 4:00 pm on Fridays with at least one other couple joining us. Halfway through the two and half hour ride, we stopped at the "halfway stop," which was Craig's creative name for a shot and a beer bar in Pennsylvania that served our favorite treat—Crown Royal. This certainly made for the second half of the ride all the more entertaining. We would play all night at The Fondue Farm, named by his friends, The Alexander's, who were the previous owners of the house. Apparently, The Fondue Farm hosted many fondue parties and unmentionables back in the 70's. If only the walls could talk!

The following morning we woke to a shot of Crown Royal to get us going and head to the slopes. After years of skiing, Craig taught me to reward myself with the alcohol AFTER skiing. That being said, we only skied until lunchtime. Following lunch, we indulged in body massages at a local spa where they got to know us well. Craig and I always loved getting massages anywhere we traveled and he was often very satisfied with the masseuses. This particular winter, he was not pleased at all with his weekly massages and attributed it to the masseuse being a "mother mucken liberal!" Refer back to "He who shall not be mentioned." Weird, because he had no problem with her the season before. His dissatisfaction with masseuses ensued wherever we traveled. I dismissed it to him feeling a little jaded by the present economical situation.

Spring came which meant golf season. We loved to golf together and managed to play about four times a week. This particular spring and summer, he was slightly burdened with backaches, though he wasn't much of a complainer. Through most of the summer, he sent me out to many of his golf outings with his buddies stating he had work to do. If nothing else, that should have been my clue something was wrong! But, instead, I embraced all the golfing opportunities I had that summer since, as a school counselor, I didn't work.

Bike rides and walks with Craig slowly lessened and ended that fall. He complained his ergonomically friendly, plush and made-for-a- man-comfortable bicycle seat really hurt his nuts. He was often numbed after even a short bike ride. I even went back to the bike store and bought him the best, most comfortable seat they sold. Still, he was in pain and discomfort, not to mention his back was really hurting all the while, too. But, he was getting acupuncture and massages at the same practice where the doctor was watching his PSA rise to 420 that August. None of those highly experienced and educated doctors put together the backaches and prostate issues. In fact, I later learned, his 85-year-old doctor was treating this rising PSA with testosterone shots and human growth hormones. Much like putting a fire out with bottles of tequila and rubbing alcohol!

Of course, my husband, the infinite believer, trusted his doctor, as they not only had a doctor/patient relationship, but also a business and social relationship that spanned for over twenty-five years. Craig opted for this holistic medical care over the conventional care after watching his father die from a long, painful battle with cancer where Pharm-Corp claimed him first, in my husband's eyes. Dr. F., who began his career in the conventional hospitals, also became discouraged with Pharm-Corp and opened his own preventative medicine group. The doctor also owned a little island that had its own little post office and Craig's company printed his stamps for him. The island was private with a membership much like our country club. His partner, John, had a boat and this club membership, so Craig and he spent many years partying with the doctor.

Yes, trust was one of Craig's assets...and downfalls. Unbeknownst to me, Craig had conversations about this rising PSA that summer with two of his buddies who repeatedly attempted to encourage him to get a second opinion. No can do. Craig trusted his beloved doctor and believed this, too, shall pass. Sometimes my husband's infinite faith and optimism showed in the form of stubbornness to those of us who really knew him. I know this still bothers his two friends as his cancer may have been avoided had he listened to them. But, we simply can't do the "If only" and "What ifs" in life; now, can we?

After much encouragement, however, from his best friend, Paul, Craig finally agreed to get an MRI for his back on Tuesday, November 13, 2012. Three hours after the test, they called Craig back and told him to get to the hospital immediately as there was something very wrong. Thus begins the very long, painful cancer roller coaster ride that lasted two years and two months.

Paul drove both of us to St. Vincent's Charity Hospital in Cleveland and having been a frequent flyer there, himself, ensured Craig got the best room with the best care. The following morning the back surgeon, along with the oncologist and urologist, told Craig he had prostate cancer, which had metastasized to most of his bones nearly paralyzing him! Despite all of these people frantically explaining the circumstances, Craig assured them all he was fine and didn't have cancer because he had been under the care of his doctor for his prostate for one and half years. It took a few more revisits by the doctors and serious conversations to convince Craig he had stage IV prostate cancer.

Craig remained in the hospital a few more days while the team of doctors mapped out a treatment plan for him. The cancer ·was too far advanced for chemotherapy to be of any value; however, radiation would be prescribed solely for the sake of preventing paralysis. Evidentially, the cancer was so entwined around his spine, having fractured many of the vertebra and rib bones, the doctors feared one wrong move would paralyze him for life. Thank goodness, he didn't ski or golf that past year!

A week later, once Craig came home, my stepdaughter, Jessica, Craig's Pastor and I picked up his completed medical report, which included the results of several tests and scans. "Malignant" seemed to be the popular word throughout the report. We knew it was bad. I made the one mistake of researching Craig's *Gleason Score* of 8. This score determines the severity of the prostate cancer. Craig was a high achiever on this one as a score of 8-10 (the highest) indicated a highly aggressive cancer. I read on to learn this score is also indicative of longevity; Craig's being up to two years. Given his PSA rose a year and a half ago, indicating cancer was present then, Craig probably had six months to live. I shouldn't have read that and vowed not to research any more of this disease on the Internet.

Thanksgiving was a bit of a blur. Craig was highly medicated, his two children were home and my entire family was present. The pictures taken that day clearly showed his pain and discomfort, but he trudged through the occasion like his usual champion self. I was on family leave and took on an active role as his caregiver, a roll I would have for the next two years. Friends and family swarmed our home with flowers, food, love and comfort, and a whole lot of *Believe* gifts! Pastor Mark and his wife, Beth, from The Old Stone Church made many visits to help Craig and I process the diagnosis and circumstances. We just remained as upbeat and oblivious to the circumstances as we could. I followed Craig's lead.

I recall only one time that I cried during this rather turbulent time. Pastor Mark and Beth were visiting and I stepped out to pick up Craig's prescription, more painkillers, which became an integral part of his treatment plan the remainder of his life. On the way home, I was suddenly overcome with emotion, choked up and ready to explode with several days worth of tears. I finally allowed the release and found myself nearly crashing into oncoming traffic. Driving while having a breakdown...is not advisable. I quickly turned into a dead end development and allowed myself to cry and scream a few more minutes, until a text from my dear friend, Mary Pat, offering to bring food, popped up. I immediately sat upright, smiled and said aloud, "Mmmmm...mmm. I love cheesy potatoes!" Cheesy potatoes always ease the pain.

Two weeks and a day later, Craig called his doctor, the one who had been watching his PSA steadily rise over the past year and a half. He asked the doctor what he was thinking and explained he not only had prostate cancer, but also cancer all over his bones. The doctor assured him everything would be ok and he had the perfect cancer treatment plan for Craig. He scheduled Craig to see him in one week. However, two days later, Dr. F., the man Craig trusted whole-heartedly, suddenly died. The strangest part of this is while this man lay dead and alone in his home that particular morning, the oncologist at the Cleveland Clinic was looking at Craig's lab results screaming to us, "This doesn't happen! This PSA (2000) isn't even a number! This is a gross malpractice suite!" Timing is everything.

I tried to keep my upbeat attitude and not only be Craig's caregiver, but also his number one cheerleader. I gathered pictures from his friends and made him a special book of memories I entitled, *Don't Stop Believing*, sound familiar? I also made a video mirage of memories playing to that very song by Journey. I played it for him many times to keep his spirits up. Friends wrote beautiful memories they each had of Craig and explained his significance in their lives. These pages were given to him with the book. He was truly touched and moved from the gesture. Go, Craig, Go! You can do this. WE ALL BELIEVE!

Craig began his radiation the first week of December and graduated ten treatments later. Somehow, Craig was able to muster up the strength still to have his two different Christmas parties at Johnny's the next two weeks. He even managed to entertain different groups of friends at a Cavs game, the Transibberian Orchestra concert and our ski home in New York for New Years Eve. He was determined that, "This, too, shall pass!" He was also convinced much of the cancer shown on his bone scan was simply arthritis. Thus began Craig's denial of the circumstances, which ultimately gave him two more years of life than he should have had. Gotta Believe!

Chapter Six
We Were Given Hope

*Hope is being able to see that there is light despite
all of the darkness.* ~Desmond Tutu

In the mean time, Craig and I needed to find a new doctor and practice. Although there were other doctors in Dr. F's practice, we could not see them either. They had treated Craig for his back issues, knowing about his elevated PSA, and didn't do anything about it. Craig and I each watched one of our parents die from Pharm-Crop, so it was important we find a doctor who was more holistic and preventative. Knowing we were burned by putting all of our eggs in one basket, we knew we needed to have a well-rounded team for each of our medical needs.

The first doctor I tried was located in a storefront and was an ND, not an MD. Nice enough lady, but that wasn't going to work. We then found the world famous, Dr. Nemeh, who was not only a spiritual healer, but also practiced Meridian Acupuncture using AC/DC currents to open up the body channels and cleanse the system. Craig immediately connected with this man and felt healed physically, mentally and spiritually after each visit. Dr. Nemeh managed to help me with my MS, as well. People from all over the world came to see Dr. Nemeh and we were lucky to have him located right in our suburb.

In February, I sought another intervention doctor, who spent two hours with me during my first visit. About thirty minutes was about me, and the rest, about Craig who wasn't even present. She inquired about stress and I calmly mentioned my husband's terminal illness, though claiming I am not a "stressed out" kind of person and I was handling the circumstances just fine. Denial wasn't just Craig's MO! Dr. T knew of a treatment from Panama that a number of her own patients were undergoing. She explained the medication and program would be done in the comfort of our home, there were minimal side effects and it cost about $20,000—not covered by insurance, of course. This all sounded too good to be true. She also mentioned it would require a bit of a life change, as he would have to partake in a very restricted diet. No problem.

I went home and eagerly explained this miracle of an acquaintance. We spent the next few days researching the program, visiting with this doctor, talking to the Panama doctors and completely buying into the entire concept. Why not? We had nothing to lose. The Cleveland Clinic could do nothing for us and University Hospital concurred with them. They gave him a dose of hormone therapy that had awful side effects for the next six months, so Craig was never going to do that treatment again. His cancer was too far advanced since it was detected so late. The conventional doctors simply could keep him comfortable.

But, not the Delta Institute from Panama. They gave Craig and me all the hope in the world! After reviewing all of his blood tests, scans and medical reports, they could give Craig a ninety-seven percent chance of full recovery. Not Remission. Recovery! This medication was going to kill off the cancer, kill the poisoned mitochondria and rebuild healthy cells. We would start on the first of April and spend a year under their care. Because the program was not FDA approved, we went by it through a "Membership." Another country club! There was only one itty-bitty thing. This restricted diet not only forbade white flour, white sugar, most meats, citrus fruits and all processed foods, but also, ALCOHOL!

What? Do you not know us? We are Team Kellem—the party couple. Alcohol was an integral part of everything we did each weekend: Golf. Drink. Ski. Drink. Baseball game. Drink. Concert. Drink. See the pattern? Craig was my drinking partner in crime. I loved drinking with him and decided I, too, would have to take on this restricted diet. I couldn't imagine eating tasty food and drinking while my husband was stuck with tofu, kale and water for the next year. We were on this journey together!

So, of course, we had a huge party to celebrate our one-year sober treatment tour. It was a night to remember if only any of us could! Over 100 people attended what began a series of parties and celebrations for the next two years, this being our last on alcohol. Thankfully, we had really good friends who were willing to drink for us during our hiatus.

The next day, I cleaned out the cupboards and locked our wine cellar. I'm not going to lie; I kissed good-bye the bottle of Crown Royal. I knew deep down this new alcohol-free lifestyle was going to benefit both Craig and me. My left leg, slightly debilitated from my MS, was doing a jig. This is going to be good for us, but what the heck were we going to do on the weekends?

After the initial shock to our bodies wore off given a few weeks of rice, greens and water, we both felt disturbingly great. At this point, Craig lost fifty pounds. Not the ideal way to lose unwanted weight, but he looked good! What a life change this had become, a good one for both of us. Apparently my MS, more importantly, my left leg, "Nelly," responded very well to an anti-inflammatory diet. Damn it. Not only that, but also, my thermogram (breast imagery test that detects cell malfunction before it becomes a tumor) results indicated a lymphoma inflammation that stood dormant for four years under the care of Dr. F. was suddenly gone. I never even realized I had a mass until my new doctor brought my old results to my attention. Maybe the previous doctor of ours should have retired ten years prior.

It was quite a discovery as I learned all the fun events we could attend, parties we could host and friends we could still associate, without a drop of alcohol. We took our friends to all of the major sporting events, enjoyed several musicals, attended wedding receptions and visited the Lake Erie islands. We celebrated at Hooleys, music festivals, reunions, concerts, our birthday parties, pool gatherings and cookouts. And, we traveled…all sober! Not even a tasty taste. Not a drop. Nothing!

We were enjoying some great new dishes thanks to my dear friend, Bick who became our personal cook. She made us our weekly meals and delivered them each Sunday. Rice, tofu, vegetables, vegetables and more vegetables. She was a heck of a cook and a baker and became quite creative with her dishes given the limited ingredients we could ingest. After about two months of this, I felt pathetic. I accept I am domestically challenged, even still laughed at my husband telling me years ago the only thing I ever had to make him for dinner was "reservations." Funny guy! Come on, I could do olive oil, veggies and Uncle Bens Rice, couldn't I? Bick gave me the hope and faith to believe I could feed my husband, thus began my own little journey within our journey as I was finally using our kitchen for something other than entertaining. Craig was so amused he even bought me some convection stove thingee on an infomercial. Because we ordered right then and there, we got this $39.95 device PLUS another one for free, along with pans, lids, strainers, all for free...$189.00 later. My dear husband believed in me. God love him!

Another big change that resulted from our new life style was I took up running. It had been about thirty years with two short intermissions once when I was thirty and did two 5ks to see if I could still run and again when I ran a half marathon at the age forty. I was happy with my times both occasions, but quickly retired each season, the latter because I was slowly discovering my left leg doesn't do well under stress. I began this new lifestyle the first of April, saw Dr. Nemeh for his miracle work on Nelly on the fourth of April and began running on the fifth. The competitive spirit I had as a track and cross-country runner was awakened and excited. I ran several 5ks and won in my age division: old lady. I was competing with my sister eight years my junior and we were kicking butt! But, all good things must come to an end as I snapped my piriformis on the Fourth of July and again had to retire my running shoes.

The biggest test was our traditional summer vacation. Each year Craig and I would fly into some city, get a rental car and explore the neighboring cities, beaches and states. Our trips consisted of beach walks, poolside drinking, checking out the towns, happy hour, fine dinners and nightcaps. Not this year. We landed in Savannah, Georgia and drove up the coast hitting the Carolinas, Virginia Beach and the Jersey Shore. Craig was a genius! He realized when the sun went down (happy hour) we were now sober and could venture to our next beach as a result. So, every few days we jumped in the rental car and headed to a new beach on our new sober coastal vaca. We had a blast! We met up with Coach's younger mentorees (Dean, Dylan and Forrest) in the Carolinas and were able to go to a tiki bar with them...sober. Who would have thought! Miracles never cease!

Craig certainly had a new leap in his previously staggered step! He had hope! He had a new team of doctors who believed in him and had just the right treatment to cure him. Dr. Nemeh continued to do the Meridian Acupuncture on Craig about every two months and Craig returned each time more moved and hopeful than the last time, if that was even possible. He had a true connection with Dr. Nemeh, who seemed very invested in Craig and interested in this treatment from Panama. He was certainly more open minded than the doctor at the clinic who quickly lost Craig as a patient the minute he told Craig, "You will be the 3% who doesn't survive the Panama treatment!" Finger pointed in each of our faces, he repeated the statement twice in case we didn't catch his skepticism the first time. We didn't need that kind of negativity and chose never to see that doctor again.

We did find a nice oncologist at University Hospitals who was open to any treatment we were doing outside of his care. After all, there really wasn't much he could do anyway other than another form of hormone treatment. Unfortunately, Craig was adamantly opposed to the hormone treatment due to the intense adverse effects it had on his body. It was no quality of life being chronically fatigued, having hot and cold flashes, and feeling overly sensitive and emotional. He cried at a SyFy movie once! Yep, the hormone treatment he was given in November put my husband into full menopause. I had so much to look forward to in the next few years when it was my turn. Though the Lupron side effects lasted in his body until May, the Panama treatment he started in April made him feel good.

With this Panama treatment, came a new role for me, not only was I Craig's wife and best friend, but also his advocate per Panama. I actually had to sign the contract stating I would advocate for Craig ensuring he does exactly as instructed in the plan, including diet restrictions, exercise, proper intake of their medication, daily oxygen intake and blood tests when instructed. I took on this role with pride and improvised.

Craig gave me new "Advocate" nicknames throughout that year of treatment:

Madvocate: When he wouldn't exercise as instructed.

Sadvocate: When he was too tired to play with me.

Badvocate: When he made poor choices and I gently remind him otherwise.

Gladvocate: When he cooperated fully with any requests of mine.

Chapter Seven

We Gave Others Hope

A kind gesture can reach a wound that only compassion can heal.~Steve Maraboli

I do believe part of Craig's optimism and positive attitude came from within, as he always believed good would come from bad and "this, too, shall pass." He had always been a very upbeat, gregarious and jovial man. However, I also think some of his perseverance came from all of the love and support he received from so many people, friends and complete strangers alike — much thanks to social media. I was an avid Facebook user and quickly started posting our journey, often expressing gratitude, happiness and optimism throughout. In February, just a few months after his diagnosis, Craig's friend, Harry, suggested we just get all of his friends together to show up at an establishment and greet him with some love and support. Thus began the "Love Mobs!"

Harry and I reached out to our family and friends and simply instructed them to come to one of Craig's favorite establishments, The Tradesman, which would become the home to many more celebrations throughout his journey. Harry, his wife, Denise, and I planned a double date and agreed to dine there at 6:00 pm. It was funny because as much as my husband enjoyed the "shot and beer" kinds of establishments, when it came to dinner, it was Johnny's or some other fine dining venue. Craig loved fine dining and wasn't clear on why I would agree to meet our friends at this bar for dinner. Being the easy-going spirit he was, however, he agreed and we dined.

At 7:00 pm exactly, one of the most beautiful, uplifting and special experiences occurred. The bar manager, Michelle, a dear friend of Craig's that he affectionately referred to as his "girlfriend," changed the juke box to our new theme song; Journey's *Don't Stop Believing*. In came over 100 people, single file line through the back door and right to our table. One by one, they just greeted Craig with hugs, kisses, words of encouragement and love. My family, his accountant, friends from all walks of his life, employees, business partners, students of mine; oh, the list goes on and on and on. We were both emotionally taken aback by the outpour of love by so many different people. I don't think Harry or I had any idea how this event would pan out, especially since we simply invited people two days earlier. Who knew a simple email asking people to just show up and walk in to a bar would change the lives of many from that point on. Craig was beaming, crying and uplifted to the highest level after the event. I don't think he realized all the lives he affected over his fifty-seven short years of life, but he would be reminded many more times after. Our "Craig Mob" was a huge success!

All who participated and many who saw the results on Facebook loved the concept. Harry was a genius! Another friend from high school thought we should do the same for our high school classmate undergoing breast cancer. I was still calling it a Craig Mob, but realized it wasn't fitting if we do it for others. Our friend, Liz, quickly came up with the term, "Love Mobs" and it took off! A different establishment and a different guest of honor, a love mob was held for our friend, Brigid. Oh, she was so surprised and beamed all afternoon!

The joy of the love mobs was that people could stick around and visit if they wanted. It cost nothing but a smile and a hug to the recipient. No gifts, no donations and minimal time. My sister, Judy, created a love mob CD composed of very inspiring and uplifting songs from many genres, *Don't Stop Believing*, being the first song, of course! I added my children's Mind Over Matter book entitled, *Love*, and we threw in a teddy bear for good measure. We repeated the concept for my former student and dear friend, Shelley a month later, though she caught on to my antics and knew what was happening before 100 people mobbed her with love again to Journey's *Don't Stop Believing*. We then had a love mob at my school for my colleague's 4-year-old son. We also ended up in the local newspaper for our love mobs. We were reaching out and helping everyone else on their journey, which in turn was lifting Craig even more!

Then we were embraced with another love mob in March, on Easter, the day before we embarked on our one-year alcohol free journey. We came to church, our usual late selves, only to see our pew surrounded by friends and family, many of whom were either of a different denomination or non-churchgoing altogether. Our loved ones gave up their Easter to mob Craig with love. Again, Craig and I were moved to tears by the outpour of love and support. These mobs provided Craig the fuel he needed to recharge and plunge forward. We believed, we were optimistic, we could beat this and we will reach out and help others believe, too! It had naturally become our mission.

One of my little sister's classmates had a wife with aggressive breast cancer. Craig became their coach and helped them get involved with this hopeful treatment from Panama. They lived in South Carolina, called Craig often for advice and ultimately became friends with him without ever meeting him. They wanted to wait until the summer when the kids were done with school to undergo this treatment. Unfortunately, this was too late. The few months in between allowed the cancer beast to spread her ugly self throughout Lori's body. By the time she arrived for treatment, there was little they could do. She died shortly after, leaving a 38-year-old father of two, who was living far from his family and childhood friends. Craig soon became his coach through the grieving process and we were finally able to meet John at Lori's service they had back home in Cleveland. Craig served as a coach even to those he didn't know.

We really believed in this Panama treatment and tried hard to encourage others to stray from the conventional Pharm-Corp treatment that we felt was just a moneymaking business for hospitals in the U.S. "There ain't no money in the cure."

Our country would be financially devastated if we actually cured cancer and had a treatment. The Panama doctors offered a ninety-seven percent chance of a full recovery, not remission. This was a one-year treatment that was saving lives in twenty-two countries, the leading treatment in China, and of course, not FDA approved in the states. As Chris Rock once said, "They are still kicking themselves for curing polio!" We'd rather save our economy than the lives of the innocent. Seems like a bad George Orwell book.

No one really bought into Craig's treatment program despite our semi-expert sales approach. We lost a few more friends and even his brother passed to the conventional treatment method. Heartbreaking! But, we still believed and Craig was determined to be an example to others. We dreamed of fundraising $20,000 for every person that we knew who became afflicted with cancer. Imagine monies going directly to the care of the patient rather than padding the pockets of moneymaking organizations.

Coincidentally, I became disenchanted with the *system* years ago after raising hundreds of thousands of dollars for ACS (relay for life, leukemia society) and The Komens. I had a student who had two younger siblings with cancer. The family was about to lose their home due to the $80,000 they accumulated in medical bills. I kindly called ACS and asked if I could have some of my hard-earned donations back for this family. The courteous lady explained that is not how it works. I kindly explained I just wanted the money from the Relay for Life that had been advertised each year as "money that will go right back to your community!" I further explained these parents were community members and needed the money. The nice lady again explained the money never goes to the people. I then stated, "So the money goes to the wealthy doctors and researchers while families lose their jobs, homes and lives to cancer." Bye-bye, *societies* of any sort. As a result, I have spent my last twelve years fundraising and donating to people and families only.

Ok, enough of my political rant, Craig was feeling and doing well throughout this year. The journey I posted on Facebook would unknowingly help people who were going through all sorts of challenges and adversity to *believe* they would persevere. One day, while I was at my new school, an unfamiliar face greeted me. I introduced myself to which she immediately asked if she could hug me. What? *"I don't even know you,"* I thought. But, I'm half-Italian, so I'll take a hug from anyone! She embraced me and explained although we are not friends on Facebook; she has been able to follow Craig's journey through my posts on her friend's newsfeed. She was battling breast cancer and having a difficult time, but because of Craig, she was inspired. Presently, she is cancer free and doing well. Yay!

Heck, we were so full of love and inspiration; we even adopted a dog from the APL. Ok, I slid this one in as a birthday gift to Craig thinking a puppy would keep him company while I went to work. I believed this would be really therapeutic for Craig, only to discover, our little Pit Bull, who I creatively named, Bella Eve (Believe), was more therapy to me. We took Bella from the hood and gave her a nice life in the 'burbs. It turns out dogs somehow develop the owners' personalities and little Bella became the child I never had: obnoxious, outgoing, VERY social, loving and cuddly, and did I mention, obnoxious.

What a treat this little puppy turned out to be. She became my PR buddy promoting Craig's story on Facebook. Everyone loved Bella…except those who met her and were clearly annoyed by her need to jump on them and be in their face whenever they visited us. Did I mention, obnoxious?

Chapter Eight

He Took a Risk

*Living with fear stops us from taking risks,
and if you don't go out on the branch, you're never
going to get the best fruit.* ~Sarah Parish

Our one-year Panama treatment continued and Craig felt great. We had a few more love mobs for him, vacationed, enjoyed life to the fullest and made the best out of the year. We were blessed. There was only one itty-bitty issue: his cancer indicator numbers weren't exactly where the Panama doctors hoped they would be as we approached the end of this program that upcoming April. Although his friend, Paul, repeatedly begged him to try Cancer Centers of America, Craig's stubbornness prevailed. He was confident this Panama program was and would continue to work.

They gave us options: we could continue doing the same thing for another year and additional $20,000 or for only $10,000 (plus living expenses and transportation); we could head to Utah where they have an alternative clinic to treat patients more aggressively. They explained we would live in Utah for a month, stay at a Residence Inn and commute to their clinic daily, five days a week, for a month. The treatment would involve hyperbaric chambers of oxygen, enhanced air therapy, far infrared sauna, resolving bioelectric depletion and magnetic and radio oscillators. Quite honestly, I didn't fully understand what all of that meant. But why not? Craig wanted it and I was his official advocate, so Utah here we come!

Once again, a party ensued in the form of a love mob to send us off on our next journey. Bella was going to stay with our friends, Lidia and Pat for the month, as Lidia loved Bella and Bella loved her. We packed our bags and moved to Sandy, Utah right outside of Salt Lake City. I was again on family leave and at my husband's side for this next step in his journey. I had no idea what to expect, but I was optimistic.

The first day we showed up bright and early to the clinic where the receptionist explained he would be there about eight hours each day and there would only be small windows of time when I could see him. Time to insert a little secret about myself. I'm very hyperactive and don't sit well, so sitting for eight hours in a tiny clinic waiting room was clearly not in the best interest of anyone at that clinic. Thankfully, I am also self-diagnosed OCD and need a routine.

So, by day two, we had our routine:

➢ 7:00 am - Wake up and get free deluxe breakfast in hotel lobby. They had all the fixings our still restricted diet allowed.

➢ 8:30 am - Leave for the clinic, which was ten to fifteen minutes away in Riverton, Utah.

➢ 8:45 am - Arrive. I would hang out with Craig for a few minutes waiting for him to get set up with his first of several treatments.

➢ 9:00 am - Head to yoga. Said no hyperactive person ever! Thank you, Jen G., for suggesting such a valuable exercise for me. This would change me for life!

➢ 10:00 am - Head back to clinic and check in on Craig. Usually he was in the hyperbaric chamber and couldn't talk, but we would wave and blow kisses and I would be on my merry way.

➢ 11:00 to 1:00 pm - Walk anywhere: to the conveniently located golf course 1.6 miles away, to the salon, through neighborhoods, to the park...I just walked.

➢ 1:00 pm - Return to the clinic and check in on Craig. Usually he was either in the sauna or on the exercise bike where they were monitoring his oxygen intake and outtake. We would visit for a bit.

➢ 2:00 pm - I would walk again...anywhere.

- ➤ 3:00 to 4:00 pm - I would return to the clinic where Craig was finishing his treatment.

- ➤ 4:30ish - We would arrive back to our extended stay hotel, have a snack and Craig would take a two-hour nap, as this treatment was pretty demanding on his body.

- ➤ 4:30 to 6:30 pm - Guess what I would do? Take a walk. Again.

- ➤ 6:30 pm - I would wake Craig up eager finally to have human interaction and my playmate back. We would swim and go in the hot tub. He was tired, but feeling pretty empowered.

- ➤ 7:00 to 8:00 pm - We would head to dinner, rarely ever repeating the same restaurant. We were close to Salt Lake City, so we had many options.

Thankfully, the weather was awesome. And, by awesome, I mean 50 to 70 degrees, which was 30 to 50 degrees warmer than Cleveland. I loved it! On good nights, when Craig felt energetic, we would see a movie. Each weekend we visited the nearby ski resorts, Park City, Snow Bird, Solitude and Alta. We swam in their outdoor pool, sat in the hot tubs and got massages each weekend. There was no schedule. We just woke up and took off on a different adventure each weekend. I was longing for Craig's companionship. He was getting fairly beat up from his treatment. It was great to be out with him having our little date nights away from the hotel and away from that clinic!

The clinic was very clean and located in a business building. The doctors, nutritionist and other staff were very kind and hospitable. The patients were friendly, but all very sick looking. Craig was the only one who didn't appear to have one foot in the grave...little did I know. I saw one young foreign man deteriorate to his death while his beloved young bride aided his feeble body, helplessly. It was rather heartbreaking and I thanked God every day for Craig's "good health." We certainly had every reason still to believe and we did. Subtle signs like hearing, *Don't Stop Believing*, on the radio, renewed our faith a few times as did seeing *Believe* signs posted in various stores. We were also blessed with flowers, cards and more *Believe* tokens sent to us from home-Friends and family reminding us of their love and reminding us to keep on believing.

We were blessed. The doctors kept giving him positive test results indicating the cancer was dying off his bones. We were hopeful. He was getting better and I was getting stronger— physically, mentally and spiritually, thanks to my newfound hobby: yoga. I never did just dip my toe into anything. Nope, once I'm in, I am all in. Each day I went to yoga classes and before bed, I would entertain Craig with my newly learned and abundant talents: Crow, sideways crow, standing pigeon and planking for up to five minutes. The latter being my daily challenge with Craig in charge. Each weekday morning he would have to choose a number between one and five, never repeating the number throughout the week and beginning fresh the following week. His number indicated how many minutes I would have to plank that morning, which was quite the challenge, as I couldn't lift a gallon of milk out of the fridge prior to practicing yoga! But, I did it each day. Thankfully, he would get my more challenging planks out of the way early in the week rewarding me with only a one or two minute plank by Friday. The weekends were a solid three minutes each day. I was determined to keep us entertained!

Fortunately, for both of us, we had some visitors to break up the monotony. Jessica and Craig's high school friends, Dave and Patty came to stay with us for Easter weekend. What a blessing! We took them to Park City Ski Resort where we relaxed with full body massages and swam in the outdoor pool in the mountains.

It was quite serene and enjoyable. It was also nice to have others engaged in our conversations. Craig certainly needed to see his baby girl and enjoyed the camaraderie of his long time friends. This visit gave him the boost he needed to finish the month's treatment program.

Toward the end of that journey, I was starting to feel a little saddened about leaving my newfound friends: The Asian ladies at the salon, the girl at the tanning booth, my yogis and new yoga friends, and the kid who worked at the golf course. I did sheepishly giggle when he said he was going to miss me not coming around every day. I only played the course once, but I bought a bucket of balls and rented their brand new Nike clubs each day to practice driving off the mountain. It was absolutely beautiful.

At the end of the month-long tour, we met one last time with the doctor. He told us what numbers to look for in the upcoming blood work and to expect a lot of pain for several months. The cancer was dropping off all of the bones, breaking the bone down and it was going to take six to eight months for the bones to rebuild. Little did I know this aggressive die off would eventually be the probable cause of many more medical problems.

But, at the time, we left with hope. We were excited to get home and back to our normal lives, whatever that had become. Most importantly, we were excited to see our family, friends, and of course, our dear Bella! The visual of Bella greeting Craig upon our arrival to our friend's home, is etched in my memory forever. The two of them hugged for minutes. Craig sitting in a chair and Bella just snuggled in his arms. It brought tears to my eyes. Despite Lidia sending us lots of entertaining pictures, videos and face timing us with Bella, it was nothing like having her in front of us. We were now home and eager for Craig to heal from his one month of intense treatment.

Chapter Nine
He Didn't Look or Feel Good

The greatest sacrifice is when you sacrifice your own
happiness for the sake of someone else. ~Unknown

We resumed our lives, me going back to counseling at the middle school and Craig going to his business for a few hours each day. He spent his first few hours of the day on oxygen, which was part of the procedure throughout the treatment. His strength started to deteriorate, as did his energy. He slept more and seemed to do less, but his spirit and tenacity prevailed. His gait changed and he was struggling a bit with steps. We assumed this was all part of the healing process.

While we were in Utah, Craig's children, Jessica and Joe both moved away. Joey moved to Florida to live with his mother and Jessica moved to Denver to teach. Craig was very proud of his children and spoke with them daily. Daddy's "Little Girl" came home in late May, and made Craig so happy and renewed. We had a nice time swimming, dining and visiting, though it was clear that Craig's health was deteriorating.

Unfortunately, Jessica's visit ended with Craig being admitted to the hospital for a blood transfusion. We later learned this blood depletion was a result of the cancer in his bones killing his bone marrow, thus, hindering his ability to produce blood. His doctor also informed him of a kidney stone he highly recommended be removed, but Craig refused. He didn't want to be in the hospital if he didn't need to be and he had a wonderful home remedy of 2 liters of coca cola and pureed asparagus that would rid him of this stone…in his mind.

I was grateful Jessica was home visiting as we spent many hours at the hospital together, of course, with all of my three sisters, father, Michael, Kim and Paul, as well. They all ended up being Craig's biggest cheerleaders and support system every time he was hospitalized the rest of his life. Even more supportive was the incredible nurse who took over the ER room demanding my husband be comfortable at all times. She was tough on the outside, but sweet as molasses on the inside. My family took to her immediately. Donna would not only become Craig's Emergency Room doctor from this point on each time he was rushed to the hospital, but also our friend. Only Craig could get preferential treatment even in the hospital. We were in good hands!

He seemed to be recharged. "Rested and ready," he would say after his new inspirational song by The Avett Brothers. We played that song a lot that summer! He was determined to get to Denver and check out Jessica's new home that June. Days before our departure, his walking and strength became so deteriorated that I suggested we borrow a wheel chair for the trip. No way! Not my proud husband. He was just fine. So there we were in the airport needing assistance getting Craig to our baggage, as he could not walk. It was an awful trip as he required much sleep, couldn't walk and was suddenly having bowel and bladder issues. The highlight was going to Red Rocks Amphitheater to see The Avett Brothers, though we couldn't stay for long due to Craig's condition. We didn't know what was happening but were sure it was just part of the healing process from his treatment in Utah. This, too, shall pass. We still believed!

This deterioration and inability to walk was especially alarming as we were taking a three-week trip to Europe in July, two weeks of it on a cruise. I suggested we cancel the trip altogether and didn't really care about losing our money. This was my bucket list we had talked about doing for years, but never did it due in part, to the great recession. But, I had saved my money, made all of the arrangements and Craig was determined still to go. Of course, Craig took it upon himself to upgrade the room I booked to a suite and get us each a seat in business class, which was like individual cubbies with everything you ever needed for twelve hours. He also found a fine Ritz Hotel on the coast of Barcelona that we would stay in for a few days after the cruise. There were no cutting corners with Craig. A bigger bonus, although we had bought into another yearlong "membership" for the Panama treatment, Craig had informed the doctors we WOULD have sugar, white flour and wine while in Europe. The man was a genius!

By the time the trip approached, Craig needed much assistance getting around so our friend, Michael lent us a lightweight travel wheel chair, which saved the trip. The wheel chair is definitely the way to travel internationally. We had priority loading, customs and treatment from start to finish. Thanks to my newfound yoga, I was super strong (in my head) and pushed him with much enthusiasm and zest. Unfortunately, our trip didn't start out favorably as we missed our connecting flight to Barcelona from South Carolina due to airplane issues. Trying to get my husband and our three weeks of luggage to a hotel in town and back to the airport the next day was not the highlight of the trip.

We always tried to find the silver lining in any circumstance and agreed to swim the next morning in the hotel pool where the airport set us up for the night. However, it rained the worst storm in years the next day with winds and rain blowing sideways at ridiculous speeds. We stayed in our bed in the hotel room ALL day and just embraced the much-needed rest from the stress of the flight the day before.

We caught our flight to Barcelona and embraced the royal treatment on the airplane. Luckily, Craig planned an extra day in Barcelona just in case there were any flight issues, so we did not miss our cruise take off. Our first excursion was to Monte Carlo, France. The excursion director explained this particular stop was not wheel chair friendly. Apparently, we would have to get off the ship and take a little boat to the shore. This navigating was not possible for Craig, so we could not get off the boat to see this fine city. Well, that stunk, but I spent the day checking out the ship, walking, sun bathing and walking more, while Craig slept most of the day. We made it to dinner that night and hoped for a more exciting day the next day.

The next day we made it off the boat and joined thirty others on a bus ride to Pisa and Florence. I quickly learned cobblestone roads were not conducive to wheel chairs and tour guides really don't care. We did everything to keep up with the group, but his chair was too wide for the sidewalks and the road, too congested with Fiats and bicyclists for us to maneuver with any speed. We were both feeling a little stressed. The rainstorm that hit us in downtown Florence didn't help our moods any. I was in tears. We had two weeks of this and my poor husband already looked so beat up. Our moods shifted, however, when our group all had to meet for lunch. Thank God for wine! Alcohol was able to bring thirty tourists from all over the world together. We had new "friends" from England and New Jersey and we were feeling cheery, so suddenly the trip wasn't so bad after all. These complete strangers now banded together and helped me push Craig down the rickety old roads, held him up when he had to stand on the walk and told their stories to us. We were greeted and helped by a Chinese man, a Maine couple, a black lady who recently lost her husband and an Australian woman whose husband was in a wheel chair for two years following a stroke. SHE told ME to, "Believe!" I was feeling inspired while Craig was in turn, serving as an inspiration to our new friends.

The weather cleared and we made it to Pisa for the second part of that day's excursion. I was able to push Craig around to see the Leaning Tower of Pisa and other attractions. I was figuring out this wheel chair thingee and he was feeling little pain due to the wine. Yay, wine! The next day we set out to see Rome, again on a tour bus with additional walking around once we got to St. Peter's Square. This would be a pivotal point of our trip, for the better. I navigated Craig to the middle of the square taking in the beauty of the incredible structures and the intricate details. Suddenly, Craig burst out crying and couldn't speak for several minutes. I thought he was in physical pain. I thought my wheel chair navigating might have jarred something in his back. I thought wrong.

Craig had a moment that changed him for good. In the middle of the square, Craig heard a voice come to him loud and clear saying, "Peter, on this rock I shall build my church!" He didn't really know what it meant, but he was overcome spiritually, mentally and physically with emotion from the experience. He had a difficult time regaining his composure, but thankfully, we just had a bus ride back to the boat and he could return to his cabin to process. Not knowing what he heard was even a passage in the bible (sorry Mom, but, hey thanks for those twelve years of a Catholic education), I was still pretty good at comprehending both the written and spoken word, and seeing through them to their real meaning.

I began to believe Craig was the rock and he had been building a church for a long time. Not only through his work as a deacon, elder and trustee at our church, but also, through his momentous relationships, friendships, acquaintances both before and during his illness. Craig had a way of bringing everyone together. The only time I saw all of his friends from all walks of his life was at our parties we hosted. All of these people had befriended one another over the years. His OSU friends were friends with his business buddies. His church friends were friends with his high school friends. He connected so many people over the years and the centrifugal force behind these people all knowing one another. Craig had been building a church for years.

Throw in his illness (and my Facebook posts of our journey), and now Craig had brought together hundreds more people. All of whom *believe*. All of whom have gained faith in their own circumstances because of Craig and his positive attitude, perpetual faith and constant perseverance. I knew what that message meant and our pastor later confirmed this and added that neither Hades nor evil will prevail. This very moment on St. Peter's Square helped validate Craig's faith. The very next day he started walking, a true miracle in my mind. He pushed his wheel chair in case he became tired and would need it eventually.

That evening, I had an epiphany. Why should Craig have to come on excursions to the next few less significant cities, when I can just go on my own? He could rest up and soak in the sun while I tour, people watch, shop, eat pizza and drink wine. The next morning I explained my thinking to Craig, who was reluctant for a nano second to send me out to these foreign cities. My lack of directionality skills and limited ability to speak Italian (hey, I got to level 2 on the Rosetta Stone) were concerning, but he luckily gave in.

I had a vision and dream of Italy since I was a child after listening to my Italian mother tell me about her trip to Italy. I simply wanted to sit at a little table outside of a cafe on the cobblestone sidewalk and eat pizza, drink wine, people watch and then shop to my little heart's satisfaction. I spent the days by myself in Naples, Salerno, Sorrento and Ravenna, only being left behind once, requiring me to use my broken Italian in the latter of those cities. Darn tour guide! I knew she would leave without me! But, I made it to the other end of the city, found another boat and made it to my ship unscathed.

Once again, I had a routine:

➢ Wake early

➢ Get breakfast with Craig

➢ Get on the tour bus

- ➢ Walk the town

- ➢ Find a pizza and wine restaurant—eat half of the pie and drink half the bottle

- ➢ Shop at all the cute little Italian stores (ask the cobbler if the shoes in his shop were made in Italy…for real)

- ➢ Return to the ship

- ➢ Bring Craig half of a pizza, half a bottle of delicious wine and some fine leather or suede shoes

- ➢ Go to the pool with Craig

- ➢ Walk the track on the top floor of the ship

- ➢ Get dressed up and go to dinner with Craig

- ➢ Be in bed by 10:00 pm

Shampoo. Rinse. Repeat.

On one of my excursions, I found myself drawn to a little, ornate, candle-lit church. It was breath taking with statues, stained glass windows, and the most elaborate paintings, I had ever seen in a church. Not only had its beauty mesmerized me, but also its tranquility. In one corner, I noticed a huge painting of the Pope with several lit and unlit candles. The area was dedicated to making intentions. I sauntered over to the mysterious shrine-like set up and said a prayer for Craig to be pain free and mobile. Shortly after I lit the candle, and, of course, donated some Euros, I left the church with a warm feeling and called Craig. Before I could say anything, Craig excitedly told me he couldn't explain it, but about fifteen minutes ago, he just suddenly started to feel good. He said his pain subsided and he was going to take a WALK to the pool. I was so choked up. I truly believe God answered my prayer and granted my intention. I do believe!

The other part of my vision and dream of visiting Italy was to take a gondola ride in Venice with the love of my life. I dreamt of this for years before I met Craig, and once I met and fell in love with him, I was determined he and I would someday have this romantic endeavor. Oh, what that man did for love! The tour guide explained Venice was no place for the weary. Craig, who was now walking free of the wheel chair, was determined to please his lovely bride. I even suggested we maybe not take this excursion together, but he knew it was a dream of mine. We didn't completely understand the scope of the city and just how unfriendly it was to the weak and disabled until we approached the first of four bridge steps that crossed over fairly wide channels. Though Craig was walking slowly, he was not proficient at steps. He barely made it up the first bridge while we were losing the group and tour guide quickly.

I noticed while approaching the second mountain of steps two men each on different sides of Craig. I thought the one was a pickpocket and was paying close attention to him. Then suddenly the two men just picked Craig up and carried him up and down the steps. I am choked up just recalling this beautiful moment. I then noticed a lady about 100 feet ahead who kept looking back at us. At the time, I didn't know this family had a system they explained when I bought them a drink on the ship days later. They were two couples from Germany. A lady, her husband and her parents. Her mother stayed with the fast walking tour guide and kept telling her to slow down, the boys stayed with Craig and me, helping him up the subsequent steps and letting the middle girl know to alert Mom that they needed to slow down. They had a system. They didn't know us. They weren't even from our same country. I was quickly learning that kindness was universal. One of the most valuable lessons I took away from this incredible three-week journey! We made it to the gondola ride and the couple from Germany took several pictures of us from their gondola. A picture view I would otherwise never have had.

The gondola ride was magnificent, but I could see the pain in Craig's eyes. He was too proud to admit his discomfort, but I knew him well enough just by reading his face. The curt tour guide approached us upon landing from our ride. She asked if we could keep up with the tour group, as she was concerned about their deadline for the boat ride back to the cruise ship. I explained we were not going to make it, I was not going to rush my husband and they can just take the tour boat back to the ship without us. There were plenty of other boats, as I learned in Ravenna (see, silver lining) to get us back to our ship. Several minutes later, the tour guide came back to us, but with our 12-year-old friend from England who we met in Florence days earlier. Unbeknownst to us (until I offered his parents a drink days later on the boat), this young boy insisted the tour boat not deport until *that* American couple was safely back on the boat. The lady tried to assure him we could still get back to the ship via other boats, but this boy insisted. So, she brought him with her again to ask us if it was ok for them to leave without us. I was unclear why the clarification, but again assured her we were fine. We proceeded to walk very slowly and I was able to hoist Craig up the steps until we were near the boats. We sat and had gelato and eventually made it back to the ship. This was by far the biggest sacrifice Craig had made for me. He endured such pain and discomfort just for me to have my dream come true.

The next day, I went back to Venice alone while Craig spent the day recuperating. Again, I enjoyed pizza, wine, cannoli and gelato. Upon my return back to the cabin, Craig indulged in my goodies. He seemed to be enjoying himself with much needed rest and some sunbathing while I was out on my excursions and then playing with me in the late afternoons/evenings. We enjoyed fine dining each night, bypassing the general dining room most nights, for some of the better restaurants on board-Craigee style!

By Day 10, Craig was ready to get off the boat and check out Montenegro, a country I had never heard of, really had no interest in visiting and ended up enjoying tremendously. This time we had a private driver and a tour guide take us in a van up and down the scenic mountain. We dined at the top and took in breathtaking sites of a white beach, blue waters, a quaint town square, and mountainous greenery. We were both amazed this 12th smallest country in Europe (out of 50—did you know that? I didn't) was so full of rich history and recent amusements, including being the home of both Madonna's and the Rolling Stones' concerts and the hotel used in James Bond's *Casino Royale* movie.

The next day, we were at sea and opted for the Chef's Table dinner, which included four couples and the chef having a 14-course meal accompanied by fourteen glasses of wine. The sea was very rocky and had it not been for the little 10-year-old, who I saw in the hall go flying from one end to the other, I would have thought my leg, Nelly had WAY too much to drink that evening. Before we were even seated at the chef's table, we had to sit in a small gathering room with Champagne to introduce ourselves. I recognized the one man as someone I had seen around the boat the past two weeks. He was a French well-dressed man, who seemed like quite the talker. I was annoyed. Craig wasn't feeling up to par, but wanted to experience this finest dining experience on the boat. Within moments of introducing ourselves, I apologized for Craig and explained he wasn't feeling well. The wife of the French man chimed in, explaining the rough seas were making her feel nauseous, too. Without thinking I said, "It's like seasickness, but cancer," to which all eyes were on me. I quickly explained Craig's circumstances and immediately we were all connected. Jon Pierre, the French man, made a toast as soon as we were seated, "To all of our new friends, especially our dear friend, Craig. May we all take home his story to our church and friends and pray for him!" Unbelievable. Jon Pierre was a gem. All of the people there were so kind.

The meal was splendid, but it was to be an all-evening experience. Craig bowed out after the fourth course, which was not even a main dish yet. He was exhausted with visions of home in his head, though he still had several days left on this trip. My new friends wanted to know more about his journey. I inspired them with Craig's story, our spirit of believing, the love mobs, his indestructible faith and his determination to live. They were in awe. They cried, they hugged me, they sent me with food for Craig. I stumbled back to the room hours later.

Our boat tour finally ended and we had a few days to recuperate in Barcelona. Not. Apparently, this is one of the biggest party cities I have ever encountered. These Spanish people went out when we were tucking ourselves into bed each night. We were on the coast and could hear everything. The Spanish didn't sleep... ever. We were in what I believed to be the finest hotel suites I have ever stayed—electronic window treatments, a shower the size of a walk-in closet with water jetting out of every wall into every orifice and windows bearing beaches on one side and the cityscape on the other. It was amazing! We took site seeing bus tours of the city with Craig cutting his short due to pain and discomfort. But, hey, he was walking on his own! Yay!

I walked the beach each day and made a rude discovery, which sadly was not the many people passed out on the beach from hours of partying the night before, but instead, the naked people who thought it was ok to expose their dimples, bulges, twigs and berries. The nice looking women and men were clothed. It was the others—those who should maybe wear a bathing suit in the shower, who felt compelled to walk naked on the beach. Divert my eyes. Now, I had a little exposure to this European lifestyle as some people on the ship thought thongs were a good look. I may never eat cottage cheese after those visuals. I found myself saying ALOUD, "Didn't need to see that" and reported to Craig throughout the trip various incidents where I suddenly didn't have a filter and may have uttered those words rather loudly. I got quite a kick out of Craig saying it when he walked with me. He would usually be a few steps behind me on the narrow track of the ship and I would hear him clear, as day saying, "Didn't need to see that!" I would look behind and he would give me his sheepish grin back, making it all the funnier. I did sleep in fetal position for a night or two after seeing some 80-year-old men and their twigs and berries. Didn't need to see that.

After nearly three weeks, we returned home. I had a renewed spirit in the human species and a feeling of connectedness to so many temporary friends from all over the world. Just for a moment in time, they inspired me with their kindness as Craig inspired them with his strength, will and faith. We returned in early August and would have a little over a month of our semi normal and seemingly healthy lives.

Chapter Ten

He Was Beat Up,
But Not Beat Down

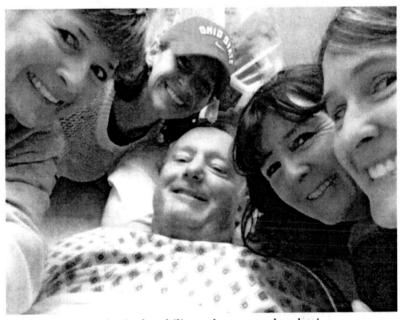

*Tenacity is the ability to hang on when letting
go appears most attractive. ~Unknown*

For the next month, Craig's walking was more painful and labored. I bought him a "murse" (man purse) to carry his belongings from the car into the home, as he needed both hands to hoist himself up the two steps to our house. Realizing quickly that even this wasn't enough support to get him in the house, I made sure I was home each afternoon to help him. Of course, he was still going into his print business for a few hours each day. He slept more but continued to believe he was healing and would get through this awful feeling.

In late August, I went back to school, excited for a new start and determined not to miss any more work as Craig seemed to be holding his own these days. That hope lasted for about a month. The nineteenth of September was a day to remember as we awoke to our usual weekday routine, but quickly rerouted when Craig let out a scream I would never forget. He was at the top of the steps and couldn't make it down as something in his hip had popped. I carefully and slowly got him to the bottom of the steps with him screaming the entire time. I put him in his office chair, rolled him to the couch and laid him on the couch while he still screamed in pain. This was so not like Craig as he had quite the tolerance for pain, so I called 911 immediately. Once in the ER, we quickly learned he broke his hip. Donna to the rescue. Dilaudid to the rescue. She did everything to keep him comfortable while my family and our friends soon arrived with their usual antics that Craig and she came to love in the ER room. He had his hip fully replaced the next day, but lost a lot of blood throughout the four-hour surgery that should have only lasted one and half hours. Four transfusions during the surgery and an additional seven while recuperating the next week, I had a sneaky suspicion our problems were bigger. Not Craig, however. Accompanied with his already heightened positive belief about his illness and so medicated on methadone and oxycodone, he started making up stories about his well-being that made even the most skeptical, believers.

Craig called his friends, and told my father, who often visited him, that the hip bone had been sent to the lab and came back cancer-free. My loving father sent out a celebratory email to family and friends excited about the miraculous news. Friends called for confirmation. Dear Lord. I knew better, but just to make sure, I actually did ask the doctor about this. He assured me the cancer was not only all over the exterior of his bones, but also the interior, killing the bone marrow. The one thing no doctor could confirm was weather the cancer was active or dead, leaving us still hanging on to the concept that the Panama treatment was working.

He was quite delirious during this hospital stay. In addition to his irrational medical stories of being cancer-free, he was also hallucinating. He told many of us about Ellen Degeneres coming to the ICU with a few teenagers from the local high school. She allegedly did a live show right outside of his room and then took the girls for a hot air balloon ride to their fall dance. He also called my sister and stepdaughter, and ripped into them for selling our home to invest in Vegas property. Um, what? We were certainly keeping ourselves entertained with Craig's creative stories!

I was officially on unofficial family leave again often working when I could. Craig needed ten more radiation treatments for both of his hips, one to be preventative. He spent the next month between the hospital and a nursing home, once again getting preferential treatment as his dear friend, Michael, was the marketing director of the nursing home. The head director also took a quick liking to Craig as they both enjoyed a fine scotch. Clearly, Craig was the youngest patient at the nursing home and determined to get home soon. We had our home handicap-proofed by our friends: Brad, his brother, Jimmy and Dave putting up a ramp to get into our home, handles on several walls throughout the house and the stair lift installed on the stairs to our bedroom. Craig had always done so much for others, it wasn't a surprise that a crew of friends wanted to help him! He was now ready to come home!

Craig settled in at home with around-the-clock care and was making progress with his mobility. He had physical therapy, occupational therapy and nursing care throughout the week. He was determined to beat this and often told me, "I'm beat up, but not beat down!" His determination was admirable. He was still pretty medicated at home, which I believe was the cause of his next hospital visit. Craig, well versed on medications and their side effects—namely constipation, indulged in magnesium citrate and stool softeners to keep regular. This apparently wasn't enough. He once again rushed to the hospital for fatigue (low blood counts) and needed a transfusion. They discovered through additional scans that he had a colon obstruction. He underwent emergency surgery and would now don a colostomy bag. They attributed the colon issue to chronic diverticulitis rather than anything cancer related. Yay! But, he was anemic, dehydrated and had low blood counts, thus, extending his stay in the hospital a bit.

I am embarrassed, but somewhat laughing as I tell you about the night he needed the emergency surgery. I was a bit out of it on one of Craig's sleeping pills. It was the first time I tried one of these doozies, and boy did it work! A nurse apparently called to tell me they needed to do emergency surgery on Craig's colon and I simply said, "That's good, call me when you are all done because I just took a sleeping pill and can't drive," hung up and went back to sleep. Apparently, they called a second time an hour later telling me the same thing to which I instantly replied, "Oh my God! I will be right up!" The nurse asked if I was ok to drive. Confused, and not recalling the first phone call, I assured her I was just fine. I slept in the waiting room and was awakened hours later by the surgeon. He asked me how and when I got to the hospital. Confused again, I explained I arrived minutes after

I received the call. He then told me about the first call where I told them I was out of it on a sleeping pill. Oopsy, daisy. *Note to self: Don't take sleeping pills when someone is in the hospital... you may get an emergency call.*

Well, the colon wasn't Craig's only obstacle. Remember that kidney stone? It had now become a larger medical issue for Craig. This kidney was blocked and wasn't doing its job either. He was not fully emptying his bladder resulting in repeated infections. Craig now needed a nephrostomy tube out of his kidney. The infections and the prostate cancer caused his scrotum to enlarge to the point where he needed a catheter, too. So, here is this debonair, classy, strong man, reduced to not being able to walk or relieve himself independently. He refused to succumb although he was slowing being beaten up. This, too, shall pass!

Chapter Eleven
We Still Celebrated

*Sometimes you will never know the true value of a moment
until it becomes a memory.* ~Dr. Suess

Craig returned to his suite at the nursing home for most of the month of November. He had plenty of visitors and quite a following still on Facebook. I was his PR manager, keeping everyone informed about his well-being as I had done since his diagnosis. Craig maintained his love of entertaining by now hosting parties and social gatherings at the nursing home. We had our annual Fall Fest party in the gathering room at the nursing home instead of our New York ski home. Every Sunday, my father and his buddies, Mark, Michael, Bob and Howie, came to watch the Cleveland Browns games. Only my husband can throw weekly parties in a nursing home.

Craig's birthday was the eleventh of November and was celebrated all week. Friends, family, acquaintances and complete strangers showered Craig with birthday cards and *Believe* gifts. His room was filled with people from morning until evening. I had a photo blanket made that included photos of over 100 of his closest friends. I wanted him to be wrapped in love from all of us throughout his illness and especially during his stay at the nursing home. The nursing staff brought him a cake and celebrated with him. I know he felt the love, I could see it on his face. I also knew this was going to be his last birthday on Earth despite my continuous, positive attitude and optimism. Somehow, I managed to push the reality of his illness to a place deep down and out of my mind.

I wasn't going to stop at just that, I was determined to continue to celebrate his life, as I had since I met him and especially since his diagnosis. I truly had no idea where he would be on his birthday, if I would be planning a funeral or a birthday party, but I was optimistic and planned for the latter. I rented the restaurant hall next to the nursing home and invited all who knew Craig to come celebrate on the Saturday following his birthday. What a turn out! How blessed we were once again with an outpour of love and birthday wishes from over 100 friends, coworkers and relatives. He was beaming! My sister, Peggy, was taking care of his medical and bathroom needs throughout the party with his comfort level being a priority. There were a few times she was spotted coming up from underneath the table with a beer bottle full of his urine as she secretly emptied his bag while he continued to entertain his friends. I can't make this stuff up! I was overwhelmed with emotion as I looked around and saw all of the people who gave up their Saturday afternoon, rather last minute, to celebrate Craig's life with him.

Craig was also determined to be home for Thanksgiving; so once again, HE told the doctors when he would be done with their nursing home services and moved back home. Again, we resumed the around-the-clock medical care and he was happy to be home with his puppy and me. We had a rather quiet Thanksgiving due to a few other family medical situations going on outside of our little world. My Uncle Pete, who was also battling cancer, was home recovering after an extensive surgery, so my aunt, cousin and her family would not be over for dinner. My father who was seventy-four going on eighteen had his knee replaced the Tuesday before Thanksgiving. Though he was quick to recover, it was a mandatory three-day hospital stay. My sister, the nurse, and her boyfriend had Thanksgiving dinner with my father in the hospital. We were down to my two sisters, and their combined six kids. His children were in town but spent the afternoon at their aunt's house on their mother's side. It was a quiet and rather depressing Thanksgiving unlike our usual festive thirty plus celebration. Craig was visibly in pain and excused himself to bed shortly after dinner. I knew this was our last Thanksgiving and saddened by its bleakness.

The next day, we were back in the ER with our gal, Donna, and Team Kellem there for support. My dear girl friends, Mary Pat and Kim, and Craig's best friend, Paul, were again there, as they had been and would be throughout each of his hospital stays. Craig was diagnosed with MRSA and pseudomonas, both highly infectious diseases that needed strong antibiotics. They recognized these repeated infections were a result of not only his bladder not fully emptying due to his enlarged prostate, but also from his nephrostomy tube and catheter. We had them both removed and Craig was reduced to using a diaper. Oh, the degradation this cancer does to a once healthy body is unbearable. But, Craig still spoke of this as temporary and that we would be on the beach in a few months.

Craig was home again for almost the entire month of December. My sister, Peggy, had taken over his medical home care. I went back to work. Kind of. Peggy got him up, dressed, fed and moving each day. She took him to his PT and doctor appointments and kept him comfortable. She was on top of his infections and treatment. She was a Godsend! Craig loved Peggy and felt she was a great nurse. I felt good about going back to work knowing he was again in good hands. I celebrated the week of December 15th when I worked my first full week since the week of September 11th. While everyone was excited about our upcoming two week Christmas break, I was just starting to settle back into work. Timing is everything!

Feeling this may be Craig's last Christmas and knowing he could no longer plan his elaborate holiday parties at Johnny's, I took the liberty to host a Christmas Open House at our home. I knew Craig wasn't strong enough to go to a bar or a hall for this celebration, so I opened our home. Now, it was not uncommon for us to entertain eighty or so people at our home outside. Our parties were always during the warmer months when we could utilize our beautifully manicured backyard that boasted an in-ground pool, full bar, cabana, hot tub and ample room for socializing. Our home, however, was just a simple colonial. The back family room, a large three-season room and a lovely, eat-in kitchen apparently held sixty to eighty less comfortably than our backyard. Thankfully, people came in shifts throughout the day! I explained to everyone this was our way of thanking them for their love and support while also welcoming the holiday season. It was catered with enough booze to intoxicate a small village.

An hour before the party began, Craig's colostomy bag exploded and I was alone completely clueless as to what to do. My sister was off on the weekends and unreachable at this time. Emily, the young girl I hired to help cater the party was dropped off during my rude discovery. Her mother, Mary Kay, immediately suggested I contact her husband, Mark, also a nurse, to come help Craig. Mark was willing and eager to help immediately. Thank goodness for small miracles. I was able to clean Craig up and remove his bag in time for Mark to reapply a new bag, even though he had never had such an experience as an ER nurse. Thankfully, he stayed and enjoyed some of the party, as we were so grateful for his unselfish kindness and medical expertise. Little blessings like this seemed to happen often to Craig. He was loved and admired, and an inspiration to many. Mark later thanked ME for the honor to care for my beloved husband. That is the kind of respect and care my husband generated from all who knew him.

Craig's children came home for Christmas and were a true blessing. Craig's body was deteriorating right before my eyes, but he was still going to, "Beat this!" His tenacity was admirable and contagious. I was posting pictures of him on his exercise bike—despite his recovering broken hip, colostomy bag, failing kidneys and awful infections. He was still going as strong as he could muster. We had our usual Christmas Eve family gathering, however, we did not make it to our traditional candle-lighting Christmas Eve service at the Old Stone Church. The only other Christmas service we missed was two years prior to when he was first diagnosed and became sick in the restaurant parking lot prior to church. This year, he knew he couldn't make the ride downtown, sit for one and half hours and celebrate with the family afterwards. We modified our Christmas Eve tradition still to include our dinner at his favorite Chinese restaurant, a tradition started pre-Kasey followed by our family gathering back at our home. It was a quieter and smaller gathering as my uncle was still fighting his own battle, so his family would stay home. Craig's body was deteriorating, but his spirit was still fighting.

His Christmas gift to me was a twenty-four hour duty-free, stress-free, night out on the town with my two closest friends, Mary Pat and Kim. They both did so much for me during these turbulent two plus years, I really wanted to show my appreciation AND have a good time with them. Oh, how I wanted and needed a girls' night out! Craig booked the Ritz-Carrolton downtown, a comedy show and pedi/manis. We set it up for the twenty-ninth of December since my friend, Mary Pat, would still be in town for the holidays. Craig wasn't looking so good and I suggested a few times that I reschedule. Nonsense. He was fine. I left him in the care of my stepkids, and with my sister, Peggy, nearby, as it was the weekend and she was on call.

The moment I entered Kim's car, I choked up and explained that our evening may very well end quickly as Craig's health was deteriorating. We made it to brunch and I actually had a Bloody Mary, but I was skeptical and knew I needed to remain sober. We walked and shopped in Tremont, a quaint and eclectic area in Cleveland. I was feeling a bit uneasy, but trying to stay in the moment. We went to a sheik bar and I had another low-alcohol drink. My stomach was churning, not from the alcohol, but from the guilt of being away from Craig and the underlying awareness, he was dying. We arrived at the Ritz and settled into our suite conveniently located right across from the suite-access-only party room laden with complementary seafood, high-end snacks and booze. I just knew this wasn't going to last.

Minutes later, I received a desperate call from my hysterical stepdaughter. Craig was vomiting blood. I told her to call 911 and assured her I would be at the hospital soon. Although I begged my girlfriends to enjoy the suite, go to dinner and attend the already paid for comedy show, they would think nothing of it. We loaded into a cab, wine in tote and headed to our usual party room in the ER. Hello, again, Donna! They all seemed to know us by now and allowed us to set up our party room without any distractions, ignoring all ER rules that clearly are inapplicable to anyone visiting Craig Kellem. Unfortunately, he had not puked blood, but rather feces (sorry) as he had more abdominal blockage. In addition, he was dehydrated and needed more blood transfusions. Donna kept his pain managed and he was in good spirits.

With this weeklong hospital visit came more infections: MRSA and staph to be specific. We brought in the New Year in ICU. Friends visited and even came during the day to wish us a "Happy New Year!" Craig and I managed to stay awake until midnight while watching a combination of his really bad TV shows and the New York City ball drop festivities. Kim had brought us plastic Champaign flutes, beads and horns. Midnight came and though we were possibly the only ones awake and coherent in ICU, we celebrated the New Year. Craig was sure 2015 was going to be *way* better than the latter year. I was pretty sure he wouldn't get to know the difference, but kept my spirits up and optimism going.

Chapter Twelve
He Still Believed!

What defines us is how well we rise after falling. ~Unknown

Craig STILL believed he was going to beat this disease. He still BELIEVED because he had the Panama treatment to save him. Unfortunately, each time he was hospitalized and subsequently incurred infections, he had to stop the Panama treatment due to the conflict with antibiotics. That didn't stop his faith! He knew this stuff was going to save him. He did a few things and spoke in ways that assured him a future of life on Earth. After all, he finally had his cabana bar built in our backyard. He wanted that bar for years, but never made it a priority. It was absolutely beautiful and tastefully done—Craigee style! He also was going to get another new Lincoln as his was a few years old. I had to stop into the local dealership and get him all of the brochures. He loved what they had done to the new MKX and was going to get another one...soon! Also, we spoke of our future beach vacations. He was determined to travel in February like we did every year. We just needed to get that colostomy bag removed and his kidneys functioning better, but damn it, we were certainly heading back to Florida and getting out of this awful Cleveland weather *real* soon. Every summer we also took a big trip. This year, we were heading to Hawaii. We often spoke hopeful about that beautiful, future trip and how we would again have to take business class as we did on our trip to Europe.

Our neighbors couldn't keep up with the activity. The ambulance visited our home a number of times since May, cars were always in and out of our driveway, parties were held and lights were turned on and off. They never knew if he was ok or not. Their indicator was our *Believe* sign I put out in November. It was an 8 foot by 3 foot high metal sign that read, "Believe," and stood with a red flood light beaming on it in the front of our corner lot for all to see who were coming and going. Occasionally a fuse would die in our garage and the sign would stand unilluminated for days until I would realize it. The neighbors often assumed the darkened sign was a message he had passed. I didn't realize that until one of the neighbors explained it to me, so I did my best to ensure its illumination each night.

I did not return back to work after our Christmas break, knowing my time with Craig was limited and more valuable. My sister was still caring for him, managing his pain, keeping him fed and encouraging him to walk every hour to regain strength and avoid a blood clot. He had been so bloated with fluids on and off for the past two months, it was just awful to see. He still had his colostomy bag but urinated on his own in a diaper. Physically, he was a mess; mentally he was still going to beat this. My eternal optimist!

Craig returned home with antibiotics, again, on the seventh of January. He had been treated for MRSA and Staph, but they felt given the antibiotics, it was ok to send him home. That evening his colostomy bag filled quickly with dark contents that immediately told even the unmedically educated something was wrong. Though I was perceptive, I wasn't practical and attempted to empty the bag using a grocery bag to catch the contents. Boy, did I pay for that one! Diarrhea exploded out of the bag, on the bed, down the side of the bed and on the floor; it exploded all over my pajama bottoms. The smell was unbearable and like nothing I had EVER smelled before. I knew, despite not having this medical background, this was REALLY bad. I was covered; he was covered and looking at me helplessly. I couldn't even walk to the bathroom to get paper towels and cleaning supplies without trailing this substance all over the bedroom with me. I returned to the bed with tears in my eyes, upset not because of the God-awful smell and mess, but because once again, my husband was being knocked down with yet another ailment. I would learn this was C-Diff, the worst of his infections yet!

For the first time throughout his illness, I completely lost it. I just broke down and cried, covered in crap, attempting to clean while I sobbed and sobbed and sobbed. Craig just laid there helplessly, in discomfort, embarrassed and clearly sick. Suddenly, I went into a fit and started screaming at God, "Leave him the F alone! What the F more do you want from him! Stop F…ing torturing my husband! F YOU GOD!" I was a tad angry. I rarely cried, let alone yelled, especially in front of Craig and certainly never to God. He looked at me as if the spawn of Satan had emerged from my body and taken over my mouth, head and heart. An hour and forty minutes later, I calmed down and managed to clean up the mess as best as I could with rubbing alcohol, Pine-Sol and Clorox bleach. The smell was still overbearing, the circumstances I knew were just awful.

I gently cried myself to sleep but was awakened three more times to more diarrhea. I got smarter and better at this, though. I wasn't going to be made a fool again! I used a sturdy bucket, had all of the cleaning supplies on hand and was able to keep the substance off Craig, me, and our bedroom. Yay, me! By the fourth time, I had it down to a twenty minute "empty and clean up" process that I still pride myself in.

The next morning, after limited sleep, however, I was not so proud about my previous psychotic fit. Craig looked at me questioningly all morning. I repeatedly apologized for my behavior and he repeatedly assured me everything was ok. Once again, I could do no wrong and had Craig's unconditional love and support. Despite his forgiveness, I still felt sick given the harsh words I used to God that evening, so I text Pastor Mark.

He immediately assured me that God was there for me.

"WHAT? No, you don't get it! I 'F' bombed God!" I retorted.

"That's ok; God is there for us when we are angry," he replied.

"NO! I REPEATEDLY 'F' bombed God using the actual word EACH AND EVERY TIME…screaming…sobbing…I yelled at GOD!" I assured him.

"God will carry you," he kindly responded.

Oh boy. Regardless of the forgiveness from Craig, Pastor Mark, and I guess God, that tantrum will never be repeated again and will possibly haunt me for a few years.

Peggy came over the next morning unofficially diagnosing Craig with C-Diff, which was confirmed two days later by the lab. Seriously, the very same evening my husband returned home with antibiotics for Staph and MRSA, he got C-Diff, too! I am not one to hate, but I am starting really to dislike hospitals at this point. I told my girlfriends I was never going back to a hospital again, though I wasn't exactly sure how that could possibly pan out given my husband's continuous deteriorating health. I never told Craig this, but thankfully, he told me that he was never going back to a hospital soon after my declaration. Yay! We were on the same page. He recognized that he came out of hospitals sicker than he went in each time. Thank goodness for Peggy, as she was able to manage his care for all of these infections in the comfort of our home. She even managed to have the nursing home doctor with whom she had previously worked, make house calls to check on Craig. Again, nothing but classic care and respect for my Craigee!

About a week later, Craig was complaining of a stomachache. His colostomy bag hadn't been filled in almost 24 hours. Again, I am not a rocket scientist, but I knew this was not good. Peggy was quick to recognize the symptoms being that of yet another abdominal blockage, but Craig proclaimed that he was NOT going back to the hospital. Ever. There was only one other option: Hospice.

Back in October, Craig's friends, Paul and Marion (also a nurse), along with my sister all broached the topic of hospice to me. To me, hospice equaled death. They are the people you call on the last days of your loved one's life to keep him or her comfortable in peace and comfort. They all explained many people actually come out of hospice and it can be a temporary solution to avoiding the hospital. How was I ever going to talk my eternally optimistic husband into such service given his denial, faith, determination, optimism, and did I mention, denial. Luckily, Paul touched on the topic first, so when I causally brought it up, Craig was completely fine with the concept. However, at that time in October, he did not need such care and opted to pay out of pocket for private care.

So, here we were a few months later, determined not to ever step foot in a hospital again. It is time for hospice. I knew what this meant. Reality, despite my denial and optimism was sneaking into my head. The kind, compassionate hospice team came in on Sunday to do the preliminary paperwork for his new "membership." From country club to hospice, oh what a change life had brought us!

Monday, January 19th, Craig stayed in bed, coherent and fighting, determined STILL to beat this. I often asked him what his thoughts were, if he was ok, how he felt about death. He did not fear death; he simply believed he had a lot more to do on Earth. For months, he would tell me, "My job is not finished yet." The last few weeks of his life, we held hands in bed and prayed together aloud. It was during these final days, I finally heard him say more than once, "Please, Lord, let my job here be done!" We would end with the "Our Father!" My husband had come to accept his death.

Tuesday morning we met the hospice doctor who informed Craig he had a week or two left to live. Craig, keeping his sense of humor, asked, "Well doc, is it going to be this week or next?" They didn't know how to take Craig. His favorite line to the nurses and this doctor was from Monte Python, "I'm not dead yet!" Although I giggled at the reference each time, while he smirked, the hospice team was not amused. Craig once again decided he wasn't giving up. He needed another opinion and another chance. We may be the only people to cancel hospice after a forty-eight hour "membership" and head back to the unthinkable...the hospital!

We spent seven hours back in the ER undergoing tests and scans while keeping Craig doped up. They were very good at immediately giving him his favorite cocktail of Dilaudid and oxy upon his arrival. His gal, Donna, would not be on shift for a few more hours, but the usual team of my family and friends, Kim and Paul, were there immediately. Craig still had his sense of humor and we were once again taking selfies of all of us surrounding him on the hospital bed. Yep, I have pictures from every single ER visit. Only my family would make the most of life in the ER.

Hours later, the doctor confirmed what hospice told him. His organs, mainly his kidneys, were failing. It was time to accept his death. It was time to dope the hell out of him, keep him comfortable and not let him realize what is really happening to him. I often thought how scary it must be to know about your impending death. I did not want Craig to spend even a minute living with anxiety or sadness. He made it this far in denial, with optimism and peace; I was not going to allow him to die in fear... or pain.

One of our last coherent conversations was when we returned home from the hospital while hospice settled back into our home. I told him I was changing his theme song from Journey's *Don't Stop Believing* to Frank Sinatra's *I Did It My Way*. He got a kick out of that and actually started singing the lyrics. I laughed and cried at the same time. This was the last time Craig sang to me.

Chapter Thirteen

He Threw a Party
on His Deathbed

*Birth is an opportunity, Life is a blessing and death
is a celebration.*~Andrew Mwangura

Here I was living with hospice and my sister, Peggy, who stayed with us for the rest of the week. This was really happening. I was saying good-bye to the love of my life, my best friend, my confidante. Muckety, muck, muck! Peggy and the hospice team upped their ante of drugs and basically sedated Craig for the remainder of his life.

I awoke with Craig in my arms the next day, though he was not coherent. The house was full of medical people preparing him for his death. Calls and texts were sent to immediate family and a few friends. I needed to face reality. I needed to step out and gain my composure. So, I did what any grieving, widow-to-be would do; I went for a pedicure. I kindly explained to the curt pedicurist that I needed her to be a bit quick about this, to which she rudely responded, "Pedicures take one hour!" I exploded into tears and cried the next thirty minutes while she hurriedly pampered my feet.

What I also needed was my heart and soul pampered, and thankfully knew just how to do it. I happened to see his two business partners walk past the salon after they had just left my home and I knew exactly where they were headed having partied with them the past ten plus years. I quickly and carefully, so not to ruin my pedi, scurried to the bar a few doors down and joined the boys for a glass of wine. We talked about Craig, the business, what they needed from me upon his passing, and basically, just how heartbreaking it is to see such an incredible, gregarious, loved and loving man have to end his time on Earth so young. He touched so many and was going to be missed by all.

I returned home to a garage and home filled with family and friends. News travels fast. Crap. The kitchen was filled with food and libations, like a typical party of ours. The kids were called and on their way back home. We spent the day in and out of his bedroom, surrounding him, talking to him, laughing and crying. His accountant, his lawyer, his ex-in-laws, my entire family, my sisters' ex-husbands, colleagues of his, colleagues of mine, his bartenders, friends from his childhood, church members, students of mine, new friends, his children's friends and friends from three different states flew in and visited with Craig for the next twenty-four hours. At one point I remember grabbing my iPad and playing a recording of Craig singing, *I'm coming home*, that he sang over the phone to me upon learning he was going to be dismissed from the hospital a few months earlier. That was a tear-jerker.

After people visited the heavily sedated Craig, they either went downstairs for cocktails or brought their drinks into our master bathroom. Several of us (self included) were in the tub crying, laughing and talking. The house was filled with laughter and tears. Oh my God, only my husband could throw a party on his deathbed!

My sister, Peggy, monitored and organized it all. She was determined for Craig's kids to be home and with him before he passed. They were due in on Wednesday, but his son, encountered delays. Jessica literally walked out of her school and got on a plane with nothing other than her purse. Daddy's little girl knew. She lied in bed with him while we eagerly awaited Joey's return home. Peg controlled the noise and energy level explaining we needed to conserve Craig's energy so he is still here for Joey. Our bedroom was packed full of people when Joey arrived home. He also laid with his father while Pastor Mark had us join hands in prayer.

The party continued after I passed out from exhaustion. Pastor Mark later told the story that he came back into the bedroom to say goodnight to Craig, but realized he was in good hands, as he saw Jessica asleep and wrapped around Craig on one side and me doing the same on the other. One of my sisters was next to me and the other two had camped out on the floor. Craig was surrounded with our love and comfort. Pastor Mark also shared how he returned to the full-fledged party in our kitchen, which included Craig's son, Joey. Somehow, Dr. Mark mentioned the Kansas' song, *Carry On My Wayward Son*, and Joey excitedly exclaimed he knew that old rock song. The group, led by Dr. Mark and my stepson, Joey, sang Craig's new theme song aloud that evening. As Journey's *Don't Stop Believing* will always be Craig's inspirational song to all of us, this Kansas' song will serve as our acceptance of Craig's death and eternal life.

The next day, Thursday, I awoke to a house still full of people. Some slept over. Some just returned. More food. More spirits. Craig lived through the evening despite his laborious breathing. My sister and the hospice team were keeping him comfortable that was certain. I don't know how my sister knew this, but she gathered us together to say, "Good-bye" to Craig minutes before he passed that afternoon. Jess and Joe on one side and me the other... I whispered, "It is ok. You can go now. I am ok. I will take care of the kids. They will be ok." Embraced in the arms of his children and me, and surrounded by family and close friends, Craig took his last breath. My dearly beloved died on the afternoon of Thursday, January 22nd, two years and two months after his diagnosis.

Pain, relief, tears, emptiness and fear crept over me. He left me.

My sister, Peggy, wasn't done with her care for him. She dismissed us all, and with the help of my sister, Anne, and the hospice team cleaned him up, made him presentable and an hour later had him laid out on our bed for one last viewing and good-bye. What a thoughtful and meaningful gesture I would be forever grateful.

Our home remained full of people until Saturday afternoon. All of his old buddies returned Friday night for yet another celebration. Harry entertained us with a long video of pictures capturing so many parts of Craig's life story. I was still in shock but a bit at peace with all of this. I was still surrounded by love and comfort. I still felt Craig's presence.

The only thing I was missing was "a sign!" I had asked him days before he passed what he was going to come back as and if he would send me a sign. He gently nodded. My mother returned as a black bird and followed me for many years, literally until the day Craig and I married. Then she stopped, but returned a week before Craig passed away. I knew she was coming to take him. I assured her it was ok as his pain and discomfort was just too much. I trusted he would be there again with me in spirit upon his passing.

A day later, Jessica and I lied on our bed talking about how Craig hadn't sent us a sign yet. Minutes after she asked me about this "sign," my car alarm went off. My car was sitting unattended in the garage. There was no reason for this alarm to be engaged. Or was there? Then within a twenty-four hour period, four digital clocks in the house went flashing. The only clock whose time I paid attention to flashed 1:22 pm. Insignificant to me until my father reminded me that Craig passed away on January 22nd (1/22). He sent me signs. He was ok. I was going to be ok!

Jessica and I later had a stepmother/stepchild bonding moment as we did the unthinkable...got *Believe* tattoos on our inside wrist. Let me just tell you that I swore years ago that I would never do karaoke, wet t-shirt contests or get a tattoo. However, a few months ago, I saw a tiny tattoo on my classy friend, Christi's wrist. It said, "Strength and dignity," and was on her inside wrist for only her to see while she prayed. I loved the idea and said if I ever got a tattoo (not gonna happen) I would get "Believe" in the same location—hidden by my watch and bracelets, and only visible for me to see. Well, add stress and death, and all my inhibitions go out the door. Jess talked me into it the night Craig passed away and the following day, I found myself in the tattoo parlor. I knew it was meant to be as the tattoo artist was sporting a shirt of Craig's favorite artist, Tom Waits, with one of Craig's favorite sayings, "It's better to have a bottle in front of me, than to have a frontal lobotomy." This was yet another sign! I am still holding off on the wet t-shirt contest and karaoke. That is a promise!

Chapter Fourteen
We Celebrated His Life

Life is what you celebrate.
All of it. Even its end. ~Joanne Harris

Despite watching my loved one deteriorate and have his dignity ripped from his soul, the benefit of a long-term illness would certainly be TIME. I had been given over two years to process, plan and prepare for my husband's inevitable death. Though I spent this time remaining hopeful and positive, I was also realistic. I saw through the pathetic looks in the doctor's helpless eyes and I read into the thought-out words they delivered to Craig and I each visit. It felt much better keeping an optimistic, unrealistic view of the circumstance than to think rationally.

But, being self-diagnosed OCD and always having to be prepared, I spent some nights in the hospital and nursing home preparing for Craig's last homecoming. Each celebration I previously hosted for Craig, felt like a "Living Wake!" It bothered me since my mother's funeral how people who hadn't seen the deceased in years, would show up to see them dead and then talk so kindly about what a wonderful person he or she was. What is that? I believe people need to hear kind words of praise and love while they are alive, so I did everything I could to allow opportunities for Craig's family and friends to tell him how much they loved him, reminisce and just have quality TIME with him.

I had time to think in detail how I would celebrate his life on Earth once he was gone. I first made him a video just of us, many selfies and all of our vacations to the Pearl Jam song, *Future Days*. If you don't know it, it's a beauty. I played that song and the video for Craig throughout the summer and during many of our hospital and nursing home visits.

I believe

I believe because I see

Our future days

are of you and me

~Pearl Jam

I also made him a video of everyone who was in his life from relatives to old and new friends alike. Though I had done one similar to Journey's *Don't Stop Believing*, after he was initially diagnosed, this one was a bit more meaningful and went to Wicked's *For Good*.

> *I don't know if I've been changed for the better*
>
> *I do believe I have been changed for the better*
>
> *But I do know, yes, I do know*
>
> *That I have been changed for good.*
>
> ~Wicked

Oh what a tearjerker that video is!

I also talked to Craig about the traditional wake ceremony I just dreaded. A few months earlier, I returned home from yet another painful wake and asked Craig to promise me he would never do that if I died. I further explained I wanted a big party with a band, full bar, food, dancing and people CELEBRATING my life, not mourning my death. He promised he would do that for me under one condition—that I promised to do it for him, as well. BINGO! We have a winner! YES, YES and YES!

A few days after Craig's peaceful death amidst a party, I went to the funeral home and a reputable party center and planned his "Celebration of Life!" I had Jessica, Joey, my father, his best friend, Paul, and my sister, Anne, with me throughout this planning, getting approval along the way. They all hated wakes and knew this was what Craig would want.

A week after Craig's death, I hosted what would be our biggest party ever. Bigger than our 300 guest wedding reception, clearly bigger than all of our house parties, this grand ballroom yielded over 800 people, two bands, endless liquor and a buffet of food.

Pictures, memory books, Craig's photo blanket and Harry's creative one hour and twenty minute video of pics entertained and allowed us to remember Craig as a gregarious man with dignity, passion, faith and kindness. We danced, boy did we all dance. Even my father came on the dance floor when the band, Crazy Chester's belted out Journey's, *Don't Stop Believing!* The singer couldn't even look at all of us without getting choked up while she sang. We laughed at so many funny stories about Craig. So many people and many humorous stories. We cried. More people. More fond memories. I tried to stay away from the criers, especially the drunk ones who attempted to corner me towards the end of the night. I had no energy or strength to console others. I was *Grieving Wife Kasey*, not *Counselor Kasey* plus I was one of the few sober people there and though I have enjoyed my new roll of being sober around intoxicated people over the past two years, I was not finding the crybaby ones entertaining at that particular time. I needed entertainment, damn it! It was a *Celebration of Life*, people, not a darn wake. "The only line at this event," I exclaimed when guests lined up to see me, "is the line to the bar!" Carry on and celebrate amongst yourselves.

I was and am still in shock over the love and support expressed at this celebration. People showed up from all walks of the world beyond the scope of my imagination:

➢ Former students of mine from various eras and jobs

➢ The members of his church of twenty-five years

➢ Ex-in-laws of his

➢ Ex-in-laws of my sisters

➢ His golf buddies

➢ My golf league

- ➤ His business associates

- ➤ My colleagues—past and present

- ➤ Craig's classmates from John Marshall High School Class of 1973!

- ➤ My former high school friends

- ➤ Facebook friends with whom I reconnected from other parts of my life (grade school, high school, college, work)

- ➤ Facebook friends whom I had never met, who were intrigued and inspired by our journey

- ➤ HIS ER nurse, Donna (ok, this is when I cried)

This was exactly what Craig would have wanted and what he would have done for me! It was like a wedding, minus the bride and groom, definitely minus the groom at this party. So many people told me they no longer wanted a wake when they passed, but instead also wanted a *Celebration of Life* like Craig. Even the owner of this magnificent hall now wanted a Celebration of Life when he passed away. One husband said he was going to do this for his wife when she passed away. She jokingly reminded him that she was two years younger than him. This made me both proud and happy, not because we were starting a trend, but because, hopefully, I would never have to attend an awful wake again. Yay!

I intentionally planned the funeral for two days later, knowing many friends may have a bit of a head ache from our Celebration of Life the next day. The funeral, which I like to refer to as his FUNeral, was held at the Old Stone Church, Craig's church of twenty-five years, mine of ten. There was an incredible turn out of friends, associates, church members and family. I previously worked out many of the details for this special celebration, again, having time these past few months, knowing the inevitable. I am grateful for my OCDness, as I don't think I could have done Craig justice had I planned it with the emotions that were with me after he actually passed away.

I have to admit, I did select every funeral song that made Craig and me cry at other services, including *Eagles Wings*, *Amazing Grace* and the song that always made us blubber, *Here I am Lord!* To add to the tearjerkers, I presented the five-minute photo video to Wicked's *For Good* that I created months earlier, which included almost everyone that was ever in Craig's life. This memorial video followed my five-minute eulogy that was probably unlike any you have heard before. Nothing was going to be standard for my Craigee's service!

I felt the purpose of my eulogy should be that all of us who gathered together Saturday were there because of one man who touched and changed us, possibly for the better, definitely for good, just like Wicked's song suggested. I methodologically identified each group of people in the church, asking them to stand and stay standing. This included family, high school and college friends, work associates, golf buddies, country club associates, church members, men he "coached," the kids' friends who referred to him as "Papa Kellem," and, of course, his fun, entertaining "Los Lobos" and "M.O.P.S." groups. The latter something he created when his buddies and he started aging: Miserable Old Pieces of Shit. They even had shirts made! Here I was at the lector looking out to an entire congregation of people standing in the church. I then stated, "If you were impacted by Craig's life, if you learned from his journey, if your life improved because Craig was a part of it, if you in any way were positively affected by Craig Kellem being in your life...please sit down!" A hushed quietness overcame the church as ALL of those standing sat down. I made my point and they were moved.

I finished by explaining how Craig had taught me patience and unconditional love. That his unbreakable faith; humbled me. His perseverance encouraged me. His life inspired me. I explained that I know Craig's life not only changed me for the better, but also it changed me for good. Sag-way into the video to Wicked's *For Good*! Not-a-dry-eye-in-the-church.

Dr. Mark followed with what would be known by all of the attendees as one of the best funeral sermon's a pastor had delivered. Not only was it heartfelt and personal, but also, humorous and touching. He touched on all aspects of Craig's life, included several anecdotal stories and inside jokes known by my family and close friends, and he sang! He actually retold the story of when Joey and he sang Kansas' *Carry on My Wayward Son* while Craig laid upstairs dying, surrounded by his daughter, my sisters and me. Joey started to sing with him from the pew and the next thing we knew, Joey was on the altar singing the song with our dear Pastor Mark. WOW! I was never as proud of my stepson as I was at that moment. I believed his courage and strength came from Craig.

His braveness shone again at the reception, which immediately followed. Again, we were surrounded by a few hundred people from all walks of Craig's life. A microphone and podium were made available to anyone interested in recalling memories of Craig. Joey asked to speak first, being the first time he ever spoke in front of a group, second to only his singing minutes before. Joey encouraged us all to cherish our memories and savor all of the experiences we had with his father. He vowed to carry on his father's legacy. This day, actually this past week, had not only physically, but also mentally, made Joey officially the "man of the house," a role he took on with pride and assurance.

After the one-hour reception, many of us regrouped at The Tradesman Tavern, Craig's favorite saloon, the home of his "girlfriend," Michelle, who always took good care of him. Once again, a celebration for Craig's life was ensuing! Journey's *Don't Stop Believing* was played a number of times on the jukebox, as was Kansas' *Carry on My Wayward Son*, again with our pastor and Joey singing together.

One of the most moving parts of this day occurred at this gathering. Our friends, Kurt and Diane, brought some luminaries we attempted to light and send off a few times to no avail due to the cold wind. Over fifty of us gathered outdoors for the first luminary lighting attempt, Crown Royal in hands, to salute Craig and say our final, "good-bye," but he just wouldn't go. We made additional attempts with the outside crowd dwindling in size as the day turned to night and the cold turned colder.

Finally, there were just a few of us out there for yet another attempt. This time the crowd only consisted of my three students, Dean, Dylan and Forrest, Forrest's parents, Catherine and Gary, and Kurt and Diane, the parents of Shelley who has battled cancer on and off for the past eleven years. All of us were related and like family after I had been the kids' school counselor years before. This particular luminary went up into the air and flew right towards and electric line. Crap! The directions specifically stated, "Do not light and fly by electric wires!" Not only did it fly towards the lines, but also, it was caught on the line. We watched in horror, hoping the flame would expire quickly given the still cold winds. Fortunately, it did and we watched hoping the kite would now disengage and fly away, but it just proudly waved on the wire, symbolic for Craig still hanging on to his life, I am sure, singing Frank Sinatra's *I Did It My Way*, one more time.

A few minutes later, we all retreated into the bar to carry on our daylong celebration. Not too long after, Catherine came running back to me shouting the kite had dislodged. I had to come see it go! We eagerly ran outside only to find the kite now stuck on a branch right below the electric wire. Oh, just like his life, Craig was not going out without a fight.

I don't know what came over me, possibly the alcohol, possibly me reading into the symbolism of the past several hours of us trying to set this kite afar, and the fight it (Craig) was giving us, but I suddenly was overcome with emotion. I walked several steps onto the snow covered grass, lifted my arms facing the dangling, now ripped and tattered kite, and yelled, "It's ok, Craig. You can go now. We'll be ok!" Nothing. I then pulled out my little urn of his ashes, reached my arms up to the sky again, and yelled in a muffled cry, "I got you, Craig! You can let go now!" To which he (the kite) dislodged and flew away in front of about eight of us. It took me a few minutes to gain my composure and turn around, only for me to see seven others looking at me as if they just saw a ghost. I think we did! That movement, that moment bound my friends and I even more with Dean declaring, "Well that just made a lifetime believer out of me!" It was the most moving, incredible experience of my life.

Chapter Fifteen
He Traveled with Me

What we have once enjoyed deeply we can never lose.
All that we love deeply becomes a part of us. ~Helen Keller

I'm impulsive. Sometimes too impulsive. Sometimes it works to my favor. That's the only way I can explain how two days after I laid my husband to rest I found myself on an airplane heading on a two-week journey: the first week to LA, California, the second to Clearwater Beach, Florida with no rhyme or reason for either location. I had a number of friends, old and new, in both locations, several of whom I wouldn't have known about had it not been for Facebook and wouldn't have visited had it not been for this journey. I just knew I had to leave town. Leave reality. Leave the now emptiness of my once filled home. But, I would not embark on this trip alone; I was taking Craig... in his urn. As sick as that may sound, it truly was a gift that offered healing and warmth throughout my journey. I knew he was not just there in ashes, but also there in spirit, and he sent me more signs.

I set off on my "Walk, Pray, Heal" journey Monday morning leaving behind a sub zero degree snowstorm that closed most of the area schools. Timing is everything! The first full day that I was in California, the Los Angeles skies were full of fog. I decided to spend the morning rewatching the YouTube video of Craig's funeral service. Within that hour, the clouds and fog parted and the sun came beaming into my room. I knew Craig was telling me to get out of the room and embrace the day. So I did! I ended up at a restaurant on the bay, dined alone and returned to my room to a phone call from Craig's friend, Dan. I told him where I was and he told me he spent a lot of time in that same area. I must try his favorite restaurant...that ended up being the restaurant where I had just dined. Wow.

After posting on Facebook where I would be heading on my journey, several people reached out and told me to stop in if I was in their neighborhood. Note to others: Don't say that to a recent widow because she WILL find you! In California, I was able to connect with an old high school friend, Susie, a former student from Brooklyn, David, and my friend and former student, Shelley. I planned just to take a cab to each friend's home, which were one to two hours away from my hotel. That plan changed with what I am certain was a Craig intervention.

About a half an hour after I ordered a cab, the concierge called and suggested I use their "car service" for such longer excursions as opposed to a cab. I concurred. The next thing I knew, I was in a limo sporting reclining, massage seats, with my new pal, Kal, who ended up transporting me for the remainder of the week—Craigee style!

It didn't take long for 70-year-old Kal and me to connect. He had owned both a printing and a marketing business like Craig, but unlike Craig, he lost his to the great recession. He couldn't believe the coincidence. We went back and forth about those businesses, the recession and the heartache it caused both my husband and him. Somewhere along the ride, I recalled him saying something about owning this limo business, inquired and then explained how my husband had also owned Silver Spoons Limo Company for about ten years. Oh, the coincidences were too much. He was divorced under similar circumstances as Craig and he loved to ski, again like Craig. I don't know which of us was more moved by all of the coincidences.

But, it got better. The first house he took me to was in Silver Lakes, about two hours from my hotel and directly around the block from his print building, which he stopped to show me. He hadn't been in that area for years and couldn't believe I had brought him there. A few days later, he took me to a clinic to meet Shelley for her first OBGYN apt. Yes, the young lady who endured a lifetime allotment of chemo and would never have children was now pregnant! Directly across from her doctor's office was Kal's mother's church, and down the street was her home she lived prior to passing ten years ago. Again, he had not been in this area in years. I knew Craig connected us for a reason. Kal was overwhelmed with emotion.

I saw my first live ultrasound that day and was moved to tears. I knew through Craig's death exactly two weeks earlier, came a new life and it was miraculously in the womb of a woman who battled and survived several cancers undergoing chemo and radiation to the limit. The doctor had never treated such a patient, as it is near impossible to get pregnant after having chemotherapy, which kills the ovaries. This baby was a Craigee-miracle! I couldn't believe it. The doctor assured her that both the baby and she were fine and not to worry about a thing. WOW!

One of my other visits was to see a former student I hadn't seen in years. He was in Redlands, California. One conversation lead to the next and I learned his biological mother grew up in my neighborhood. I knew of her from growing up and recalled how she had endured a difficult life. David and I shared how our mother's passed away. We had quite an evening reconnecting and telling our stories. A small world full of coincidences.

That Friday of my first week, I was supposed to drive up the coast in a rented convertible to see yet another old friend from high school. Craig and I often rented convertibles on our trips and traveled from one beach to the next, however, he was ALWAYS the driver. I was feeling independent and cool, but I had been fighting a bug since Sunday. Yes, the body finally responded to my two and half years of stress and shut down the day after I laid Craig to rest. By Friday, I was feeling worn out, and quite honestly, lost my confidence and cool in my ability to navigate myself to a city two hours north. This worked out well for me as I later learned San Diego was two hours south of me. Dear Lord!

I spent the morning and early afternoon vegging in the cool sun, medicated on Theraflu. Later, my friend, Susie, who was now bored, texted me asking if I wanted company. By this hour I was really getting bored myself, so I welcomed her. She took me to Venice Beach where we spent the late afternoon and early evening walking, window shopping and eating. It was time well spent as we really connected. I was learning all of these former acquaintances' stories and bonding. Something had drawn us together. The next day I set off for my usual walk and asked the valet if there was somewhere more interesting for me to walk other than the Del Ray Marina and wharf. He looked at me oddly and suggested I just walk to Venice Beach. I reiterated that I wanted to WALK, to which he explained Venice Beach was literally around the block and down the street, an eight-minute walk. Even after Susie drove me all around Venice, I had no idea I was staying right by a beach. I am so directionally challenged. Craig had certainly been my guardian angel this trip. I could hear him saying, "So many college degrees, yet no directionality skills whatsoever!"

Once in Florida, I was greeted again with clouds and rain that quickly changed to sunshine upon my arrival. My first hotel was from a chain that Craig and I frequented, however, this particular building was not worthy of its name as it looked and served more like a cheap motel. Also, I learned I wasn't quite in Clearwater Beach as I had planned. I was in Sands Key, which in NO way is even close to the aesthetic beauty of Clearwater. Don't let anyone tell you otherwise. WWCD: What Would Craig Do? He would have left to a better location and hotel, so I did just that. Kind of. I ended up on THE Clearwater Beach, however at a hotel that didn't quite have the appeal I had become accustomed. Craig created a real travel snob out of me. So, after two days at this hotel, I was finally able to land a posh suite at the Hyatt—Craigee style! I knew he would be proud of my insistence on an upgrade. At least, I kept telling myself that as I looked at the additional $600 I would incur the next three days.

In my last minute planning, I had asked the travel agent to get me on any one of the Florida beaches Craig and I had frequented over the past eleven years: Sanibel, Marco, Naples, Sarasota, Tampa, Ft. Myers, Key West, and Key Largo. But, he could only find a room on Clearwater. I was a bit bummed, as I had never traveled to Clearwater with Craig, at least which is what I thought. After I posted some pictures of the pool and beach on Sand Keys, my girl friend text me explaining that is where we all stayed for our 40th birthday celebration trip that not only included four girl friends and Kim's husband, Dave, but also CRAIG. OMG! I had traveled here with Craig after all and stayed in the SAME HOTEL and swam in the SAME POOL! Let's just say that particular trip was a little blurry as alcohol was definitely involved. In fact, we still have a running joke about Mary Pat's Coor's cooler that she brought down to the pool filled with booze and beer. Craig was appalled at the time as the pool offered a conveniently located tiki bar with the same alcohol options. You simply don't bring a cooler down to a nice pool with a bar right there. That cooler went back and forth between Craig and Mary Pat as gifts for a few years after that. We were definitely "Classholes" and he got such a kick out of all of my friends.

I had the joy of connecting again with souls I would otherwise never have seen again in my life had it not been for this journey: A student I had in the mid 1990's, a college buddy and his wife who I last saw in 1987, and sisters who moved here to be with their family a few years ago. Even better, my dear friend, Mary Pat, came from New Jersey to spend the long weekend with me. Craig was keeping me in good company! I could feel his presence.

As soon as Mary Pat arrived, she suggested we take her rental car for a ride to Anna Maria Island, the all-time favorite location of Craig and mine. He had actually taken all of my friends and me there in a limo from Clearwater when we were here for that blurry 40th birthday celebration. It seemed that no matter where we traveled in Florida, Craig and I always ended up on Anna Maria Island for a drink and a visit with one of his oldest friends. What a kind and thoughtful gesture! So, we packed Craig with us and enjoyed a beautiful day on the sunny beach at his favorite restaurant, The Sandbar. I was so grateful for this wonderful moment.

That weekend was also the host of a difficult Hallmark Holiday: Valentine's Day. My mother, with whom I was very close, died on February 14th, eleven years earlier. Incidentally, I was staying in suite number 1241, my mother's birthday (December 1941) the latter part of this trip. She was buried three days later on my parents' 42nd anniversary. I hadn't been a fan of the day since, though Craig always made it special by taking me to Florida each year. So, here I am in Florida, on that dreaded day, without either Craig or my mother. Boo.

But, once again, my friends prevailed. First, Mary Pat joined me in going to the spa and getting a much needed massage. Apparently, I had a few knots in my back and neck. Imagine that? Also, our friends, Vicki and Val, drove from Tampa to come spend the day with us. Both girls donned Mary Pat and me with Valentine's gifts, such a sweet gesture, and me, also with some beautiful Believe gifts. One can never have enough Believe signs and jewelry, that's what I say! We spent part of the afternoon basking in the 60-degree sun on the pool deck we pretty much had to ourselves and then we dined in our suite. Their company was quite pleasant and a great deterrent to the reality of the day.

The next day was my last day on my journey, and, of course, the nicest day weather-wise that week. Go figure. I was able to enjoy a walk on the beach, though I felt those knots reappear pretty quickly. I was dreading the return home to my empty, lonely home. I had done a nice job escaping reality the past two weeks, but it was time to face it all including the negative 35-degree weather, 100 degrees below the weather I was leaving. Had it not been for Bella, I may have extended my stay. Her two-week camp ended that same day, so, I knew I just had to return. I prayed to Craig and God to maintain my strength, positive attitude and optimism.

Chapter Sixteen
I Still Believe

Mind over matter: You become what you perceive. ~Unknown

I returned to frigid temps in Cleveland. Dread. But, was greeted by my dear sister, Anne. She immediately took me to my father's house to get my car. He wanted to watch some videos of my mother, as it was their anniversary weekend. While we were watching one of the videos, he asked me to show him my tattoo, so I did, but he immediately responded, "That's no tattoo! This is!" He then pulled up his sleeve to reveal the 1-year-old tattoo of my mother's high school portrait now proudly donning "BELIEVE" underneath. Bawl. I was so touched my father would add Craig's mantra to the tattoo of my mother. WOW!

Needless to say, I had a mini breakdown the whole way home. It may have been the slowest I ever drove as I kept jerking the brake pedal during my crying fit. But, I was warmed again once I got home. I was first greeted with our *Believe* sign that still stood proudly on our snow-laden lawn. Inside the house, hundreds of cards were on the table, ready to be opened and read. And, most importantly, Bella was home thanks to my sister, Judy, who picked her up a few hours earlier. Unfortunately, however, Bella was very traumatized by Craig's death and my departure. She took weeks to heal physically and emotionally, crying often and reverting back to many old puppy behaviors. It took her a few days before she could even sleep in Craig and my bed. She knew and she was grieving. My poor little girl!

Clearly throughout the journey, I did not have the time, energy or desire to sit back, soak it all in and realize fully the awfulness of my husband's horrific, debilitating and degrading disease. Thank God! As a result, I was fully capable of remaining upbeat, positive, optimistic and healthy—both physically and mentally. Now that he is deceased, I occasionally have visions of him stumbling, wincing and groaning. Each time I feel pain and disdain, not towards God, but towards the disease itself. These are all feelings I don't enjoy, quickly bury and certainly won't act upon (refer back to my tantrum to God). I am relieved

I didn't use the little energy I had on negative thinking or painful feelings. They would have been counteractive to my role as his devoted and caring wife, and caregiver. Craig was a priority and I am so glad I allowed my soul, heart and mind to be cleansed throughout his illness, so I could best serve him. My friends and family were close by always to keep me lifted and moving forward.

Obviously, Craig's cancer came to me as a complete surprise as he wouldn't even wear regular deodorant due to its zinc—a cancer causing agent, let alone eat anything with Aspartame. He knew all the foods that caused cancer and mainly avoided them. I guess what I learned is—life causes cancer. Cancer has no prejudices. It doesn't care about your ethnicity, sex, social status, religion or political views. Cancer doesn't care how healthy you ate or exercised. No, I've seen even the most health conscious people get this awful affliction. What I learned from Craig is that when cancer comes knocking at your door, as it very well may, embrace the disease, stay positive, plan for a long future despite the prognosis, welcome the love, support and help from others, and most importantly, BELIEVE.

Do I still believe in this Panama program? Sure! Why not? If nothing else, it gave my husband the hope he needed to live two years more than expected. Those were the doctors who gave him good news and hope throughout the program. Could a program like Cancer Centers of America have given him more years of life? Possibly, but I will never know or regret his decision to stick with the Panama treatment regardless of the outcome.

I also want to be clear in recognizing that yes, like many tragedies in life; none of this had to happen. He had an early PSA reading by his doctor of twenty-five years that would have resulted in a biopsy by any other doctor. A second opinion in 2011 would probably have enabled him many more years of a healthy, happy life. We can't regret and think of the "would haves" and "should haves." My husband trusted his doctor and put all of his eggs in one basket. Craig taught us many great lessons in life, some, like this, less purposely.

I am grateful, however, for the lessons taught to me by Craig. From the beginning of his illness, his eternal optimism inspired many, including myself. He lived for years with the mantra: "Believe" and was tested. However, we all quickly learned "Believe" was not just a mantra to Craig.

Believe was his way of life:

➢ He *believed* when they told him it was terminal. We were not to ever use that word.

➢ He *believed* when they told him it was on all of his bones from his cranium to his knees. Nope, that was just arthritis!

➢ He *believed* even when the doctors from the two nationally known hospitals in Cleveland could do nothing for him.

➢ He *believed* in the Panama treatment, the doctors who gave him hope.

➢ He *believed* in Dr. Nemeh's spiritual and acupuncture care.

➢ He *believed* even after they explained his prostate was so laden with cancer that his other organs were compromised, jeopardized and closing down.

➢ He *believed* he still had a job to do.

➢ He *believed* in a long life while signing up with hospice care.

> ➤ He *believed* until the moment he died.

Many people go to their graves never once having what Craig and I had for those eleven short years. People were married for far more years than we were, but didn't laugh the way we did. Couples celebrated their milestone anniversaries, though never respected one another the way Craig and I did. Spouses young and old may not have loved unconditionally and eternally, as Craig and I did.

We loved:

Through good times and bad

Through happy times and sad

Through sickness and health

Through the recession and wealth

I consider myself blessed not just because of all of the cherished memories I have of Craig, but also, because of the time I had with him, even through his illness. The unsurmountable love and support that resulted from his illness will never be forgotten. The connections I made with others battling cancer or caring for a diseased loved one, will not be lost. The confirmation that my close friends are TRULY friends who rose to the occasion showering us with all we needed to survive those two plus years will be cherished for life. I made so many more friends, lifelong buddies of Craig's, who I will always treasure and hope to continue to play with over the years. My family, the most loving, giving, helpful people I know, will always be the most important people to me. As they did for me, I will always drop what I am doing and be at their side when in need, even if it is in the ER room at the dreaded hospital. I can only hope our nurse, Donna, will be there for their care.

I am sure there are some really good parties going on in Heaven without me; and this does truly sadden me. My time will come to join Craig at the bar. I will patiently wait. God took Craig back, as he was just a gift to me. I accept this. I am blessed with fond fun-filled memories that no one can take from me. I am grateful for my insistence to capture every moment I could on camera. Those selfies, party pictures and beach photos will always be treasured.

I am not going to stop believing. I will continue my journey. Because I knew Craig, I do *believe* that I have not only been changed for the better, but also I have been changed for good!

Chapter Seventeen

I Received

Sometimes the person who tries to keep everyone happy is the most lonely person, so never leave them alone because they will never say that they need you. ~Unknown

Throughout Craig's illness and for a few months after, there were things I needed from others that I never asked for or even realized I needed. Friends, family and people I really didn't know, however, did know what I needed—somehow, someway. For this, I will be forever grateful. This chapter is for all of those who have someone in their life experiencing any hardship, as I believe what was done for Craig and me, could certainly benefit others in need.

1. **Take the person for a walk.** Kim took me for walks often. She was sometimes insistent to get me out of the house and for this, I am forever grateful. I needed the walk, fresh air, camaraderie and distance from the reality back at my home. She was there for me and it was just a simple walk that rejuvenated me, and helped me get through the rest of the day! My friend, Dawn, came over for "Ma'am cave" nights where we exercised and talked, giving me the opportunity to unwind and readjust. I desperately needed girl time!

2. **Check in often.** My friends, Christi and Bick, texted me almost daily just to see if I was ok and to ask what I needed. Every emoji made me giggle, every "Love" made me feel valued. My sisters and other friends called, texted, emailed or Facebooked me just to check in. I needed them to check in on me. That simple. To know others outside of my world were still connected to me was monumental. The roll of caregiver can cause loneliness and isolation simply due to the nature of the diseased. For months after Craig's death, several of his buddies still called and checked in on me. This warms me and makes me feel like Craig's life has not been forgotten, nor has his wife. :)

3. **Take meals.** A meal from Boston Market (Thank you, Judy) is just as good as a home cooked meal to me! I

discovered my friends were pretty darn good cooks during this time and am forever grateful for their meals. Kim brought us meals every Monday. Our friends, Katharine and Mark, brought Craig top-notch meals on Sundays to enjoy after the football games. Even when Craig was in the hospital or nursing home, the meals that were brought to our home for me were much appreciated. If your friends tell you they don't want or need food, they are probably lying like we did when people first started bringing food after my sister, Anne, set up a meal plan—best program ever!

4.   **Stay connected via social media.** I have found value and goodness in Facebook and email, especially through Craig's journey. People from all over reached out to just say, "Hello," check in, let me know they are praying for us or to inquire about our needs. I was Craig's "PR director" of social media. He was elated with all of the kind and encouraging comments written on Facebook and emails upon my daily/weekly updates. I truly believe these words of kindness lifted Craig's spirits when I read them to him each day.

5.   **Send cards.** Just to know Craig and I were not forgotten by our church family or friends near and far meant the world to both of us. Sometimes you feel like a prisoner to the disease as you are stuck at home or in a health facility. Cards bring sunshine to the cloudiest days.

6.   **HUGS!** You can't go wrong giving a weary friend or the caregiver a hug. Nothing fills your body with more warmth than another body bringing you in with comforting arms. You don't even have to say a word. The hug says it all… and costs nothing. :)

7. **Small tokens of care**. We certainly didn't need any gifts, but the plethora of flowers and *Believe* tokens (stones, bracelets, necklaces, pins, decorations) that were sent to us during this time made us feel special, remembered and loved. We received gifts from people from whom I hadn't seen or heard from in years, just to let us know they were rooting for us. Former students and colleagues of mine who never met Craig, sent gifts I will always treasure. WOW! Flowers and fruit gifts really brightened our days. So many new connections were made by these small gestures that were so huge to us. My dear friends, Christi and Bick, and Craig's partners, Mike and John, each sent flowers to my hotel when I took my hiatus upon Craig's death. I knew I wasn't alone on that journey.

8. **Bring comfort**. Craig's girlfriend, Michelle and daughter, Alyssa, brought Craig a blanket one of the many times he was in the hospital. My girlfriends, Terry, Betsy and Erin, also brought him a different blanket for his birthday. Both were very soft and comforting and varied in size. He wrapped himself in both, one around his lower body and one around his shoulders and upper body often, as he was chilled much of the time. Craig actually used each gift the minute he received them, as he was cold each time. Such a simple idea that offered tremendous comfort to Craig!

9. **Attend birthday parties and celebrations**. Even if just for a few minutes. Your presence is needed and felt. You lift the sick and needy just by showing up to the party. Your attendance makes the person feel worthy, loved and needed. It gives them just the more reason to keep on fighting.

10. **CELEBRATE with Love Mobs**. Throw a "Love Mob" for the sick (and the caregiver). It costs nothing but time

and not much time at that. Simply secure a location with the approval of the site manager, make sure you have *Don't Stop Believing* on a boom box or jukebox, and send one email for people to come. Just show up. People can come for a few minutes or hours flooding the sick with hugs and smiles. It is up to each person and believe me, ten minutes of your sunshine is just as spectacular as two hours. The love mobs definitely put a lot more giddy-up in Craig's labored walk.

11. **BELIEVE.** Stay positive, upbeat and strong for the sick. You can cry your heart to sleep when you are away from them, but in their presence, bring peace, happiness and comfort. Show optimism and faith with whatever the prognosis. It's only a prognosis and many tend to be less accurate than others.

12. **Offer your medical expertise.** If you are in the medical field and can help the caregiver with some of the basic caregiving, please do. My sister, Peggy, was a Godsend. Her expertise allowed Craig to be comfortable until his last breath. She recognized infections and other health concerns, and was able to seek the appropriate medical help, as a result. I am not a medical expert and was uncomfortable just seeing all of the tubes and bags hanging from Craig, let alone changing and cleaning them. Our friend, Maryann, also a nurse, was able to offer sound advice to us when we had off-hour questions. It was such a relief to have someone else to reach out to for a second opinion. Having our friend, Mark, come help Craig last minute with his colostomy bag was a blessing as well. We would have spent the afternoon in the ER had Mark not saved the day!

13. **Offer your skill/trade**. If you are a handy man, yes! We need your help! I promise you, something needs to be done in the house the caregiver and sick person cannot attend to or fix. Be persistent. If the individual has some new physical limitations, offer to make the house handicap-friendly. We were forever grateful to Brad and the crew who did just that for our home. From a ramp to wall mount handles; our home was Craig-ready upon his return. Those boys gave up their evening and put together their talents to help Craig live comfortably and safely in his home.

14. **Visit**. Just come and sit with the ill. Your time with them is so welcome and needed, even if no words are exchanged. Come watch the game with them just as my father and Craig's buddies, Mark, Howie and Bob, did every Sunday. Wow, did that give Craig a jump in the week! He was always renewed by their visits, time and camaraderie. I will forever be grateful to these guys all spending their Sundays in the hospital, nursing home or our family room watching the football games with Craig. Their company was so appreciated and needed. Craig also enjoyed the daily morning visits by our cleaning lady, Lidia, as she showed such respect and kindness to Craig. Who would ever think to visit a person in the emergency room? Well, aside from my awesome family, our friends, Paul, Michael, Kim and Mary Pat, certainly did. And, what a difference it truly made to Craig. We knew each ER visit was not good and would result in a long-term hospital stay, but for all of these people to drop everything, EVERY time and come to the hospital to wait and wait and wait...WOW! I don't know who benefitted more from that, Craig or me, probably me, since Craig was heavily sedated each time. Those ER visits are timely

and depressing. I am so grateful for the crew that kept us company each time.

15. **Call**. Take a few minutes out of your busy day just to call and say, "How are you really doing?" "I Love you!" "I am praying for you." "What do you need from me?" My close friend, Mary Pat, had moved away a few years ago, so hearing from her weekly was very uplifting and much needed. Although the sick and caregiver may simply say all is good and they need nothing, please know you already met their needs with your kind gesture of a simple phone call.

16. **Pray**. I'm not going to get all religious on you, but I do certainly believe in the power of prayer. We had friends saying Rosaries for Craig (Thank you, Luanne) and church groups from all around praying for and devoting services to Craig. I personally experienced the power of prayer in Italy. I know it works. Just a short little prayer asking God to give the sick the faith, determination, strength and courage to get through their illness is all you need to ask. You can certainly ask for a cure and other miracles, but I try not to be too greedy. :)

17. **Share memories with the sick.** Craig's friend, Harry, created a book with so many fun-filled memories of Craig over the past forty years. This book was treasured by Craig throughout his illness. It was a nice resource for him to refer to as it helped elevate his mood and drive to keep on keeping on. Friends who visited often, spent time reminiscing, which certainly got Craig laughing and validated his life with his buddies.

18. **Provide transportation**. Is your friend or family member getting radiation or other treatment daily/weekly? Offer to drive. It is certainly a nice way to bond with your friend

or family member and relieve the caregiver. Be persistent. Tell them which day you are driving them. My father and our friend, Paul, were wonderful this way. I would have missed work more often had it not been for them. They were able to take Craig to his radiation treatments daily and spend some time with him. Craig enjoyed the companionship and support. I enjoyed being able to get back to work occasionally.

19. **Support your colleagues.** If one of your coworkers is sick or a caregiver, don't hesitate to offer support, even if you don't really know the individual. Craig was in his second year of illness when I changed schools. I only knew a handful of people and had very sketchy attendance for much of that year, including the month-long treatment in Utah. The staff was so kind and supportive to me. No one questioned my work ethic for not being at work often and my administrators and co-counselor worked diligently caring for my students daily. I was technically assigned to the 6th and 7th grade teams, who were very understanding and compassionate to me. Teachers of the 5th graders often also reached out to me, sent me cards and greeted me with hugs upon my return. I barely knew them, but they were there for me. The entire school, under the leadership of my principal and friend, Tiffany, sent me a basket from which I am still enjoying the benefits! It included teas and tea accessories, along with a salon gift certificate. Massage? Yes, please, and thank you! Never did anyone ever make me feel like I was shirking in my duties or responsibilities. I was so grateful to be working with such an incredibly supportive and considerate staff.

20. **Keep the memories going.** After Craig passed away, several people lifted me through their acts of keeping Craig's memory alive. My father and my nephew, Joe,

both had "Believe" tattooed to their arms. I cried seeing each tattoo. What a selfless act of kindness and act of respect for my husband. I'm not suggesting everyone get a tattoo, but if you do, you certainly will touch the family of the deceased! My friends, Kim and Dave, brought an enlarged photo of Craig with a glass of booze in his hand cheering. This was put above our outdoor bar and serves as a beautiful reminder of Craig allowing us to toast to him often when I am entertaining. It is as if he is with us at each gathering. Our friends, Kurt and Diane, gave us fifty luminaries to light off in remembrance of Craig. These have served as gentle reminders that Craig certainly is here in spirit with us.

Epilogue

My vision and purpose of this memoir was to show those individuals afflicted with cancer (or any other disease) along with their caregivers, families and friends, that despite the diagnosis, and the possible impending death, you can still embrace and celebrate the days of life remaining.

I hope Craig's unending faith and confidence that inspired all who knew him will also inspire all who read this. Yes, he died. But, he lived each and every day to its fullest with faith, gratitude, happiness and optimism. I encourage all afflicted with any terminal or challenging disease to approach it as Craig did with determination, hope and courage and for the caregivers to embrace, capture and celebrate every moment with optimism and gratitude.

I am forever grateful to my father, sisters, friends and colleagues who helped me throughout this journey. Your presence, words, actions, etc., were all gifts to Craig and me that got us through each and every passing day. I can't imagine this experience without all of you and your support. It takes a village to care for a dying man and for our village, I am thankful!

A special thank you to the professionals who gave my husband hope:

Dr. Issam Nemeh

Dr. Sherri "T"

The Delta Institute Doctors

Dr. Matthew Cooney, Md., University Hospitals

Dr. Mark Giuliano, Pastor, Old Stone Church

Craig Inspired Many

"Craig inspired me to keep going - to not give up - not surrender to feelings of defeat. I was diagnosed a year and a half ago with Stage IV Renal Cancer and I felt hopeless - very down - who knew a person could hold that many tears inside? The strength and determination that I saw in Craig, as he journeyed through his own courageous battle, gave me the extra boost to toughen up and keep going. The image of his smile and encouraging words, during our last chat, keep cheering me on - Craig's determination has been my inspiration - and always will." -Michelle Hyatt.

"B E L I E V E Craig gave true meaning to that word for all of us. His belief, in himself, his God, Kasey, in his family and friends, in life itself, is a strong message to be remembered and embraced. He blazed a path through dark times and Craig came through to the light but he left us with a beacon, a message - B E L I E V E !" -Ginni Going

"Of course we all hope and pray that we won't face the inconceivable challenges that Craig did..but of course, some of us will... Should that be me, I would pray that I would face it with the same passion, class, and dignity that Craig did... and at the same time radiate the love that we all felt while with him." -Dann Skutt

"'1/2 full----1/2 empty?' When I'm having one of those days, on the course, around the house, or out and about it helps me to cope with what I like to remember as a "Craig outlook." No matter what he faced, he always had a smile and attitude that made me feel like the glass was 1/2 full and probably would be getting fuller!" -Mark DeLorean

"The heartiest of people when challenged with a terminal illness become daunted and the spirit wanes. Craig's indomitable spirits made his difficult and challenging journey a road map for

all of us. Craig was the poster child for indomitable spirit!"
-Penny Lins

"Craig inspired me to have an open and generous spirit. Because he shared all his experiences with his disease I understand how I might help others with this horrible disease. He showed me that people who are dealing with this need people around them. It's good to talk about and share what is troubling you. He inspired me to be more connected to those I love and care about. I am also a better person for having known him" -Mary Pat O'Toole

"Craig's unlimited positive optimism in business and in life before and during his illness was always welcomed and contagious. He was and is an inspiration to many. He is missed every day." -Mike Nakonek

"CWK was probably the most interesting thoroughly civilian alpha male I ever hung out with and loved as a brother...Bless him." -Larry Lins

"In the last year or so of Craig's life he spoke several times of buying/building a Studebaker Avanti. I regret that we will never have that opportunity."-Dennis Crawford

"When Craig and I parted ways as roomies at the notorious red house back in '84, he threw his arms around me and said, "Lewie, long may you run." I never forgot the look in his eye. Craig's love was evident. He was a big guy with an even bigger heart." -Jim Lewis

"Witnessing Craig and Kasey's journey through cancer has been a humble, tearful, faithful, loving and inspirational experience for us, and one we will never forget. Craig and Kasey's courage and continued belief was contagious and we were blessed to witness the love and transformation of so many

people that were also part of the journey. We have learned to never give up and to, above all, keep our faith in God, always."
-Jen and Joseph Guiliano

"Craig was always a very positive person during good and bad times. Over the years we have had the best of times. He will always be remembered." -John Gergel

"Craig taught us how to face life's greatest challenge with strength, dignity, faith, humor and, most importantly, a strong belief in surrounding one's self with loving and supportive family and friends." - Cindy Miller

"As a friend for 35 years I found much to admire about Craig as a man. However, one of the traits I found most impressive was his ability to hold friends close and always make you feel special no matter your flaws or station in life. If you were his friend you were his friend forever and the benefit of that was you were included in much of his life. He was smart, he was strong, he was fun, he was generous and I feel sure his spirit will hold all his friends close to him forever. I cherished his friendship, I miss him and I think of him often." -Jeff Miller

"While not having known Craig for as long as others, I found him to be a spiritual man. He accepted things as a matter of fact, he lived in the moment and was forever grateful for those around him while always remaining courageous and faithful."
- Tony Gallo

I have a Craigism he told me many years ago and I have followed it for a very long time. Craigism #32: " Don't do what you can't do well. Hire someone who is good at that task. You do what you are good at."

Another Craigism. He followed this one since I've first met him back in high school. Call it Craigism #1: "One hand washes the other" -Kevin Becker

CPSIA information can be obtained
at www.ICGtesting.com
Printed in the USA
FFOW05n1251230815

9 781612 443799